DISCOVERING THE PARABLES

An Inspirational Guide for Everyday Life

HENRY G. COVERT

Westport, Connecticut
London

Library of Congress Cataloging-in-Publication Data

Covert, Henry G.
    Discovering the Parables : an inspirational guide for everyday life / Henry G. Covert.
      p.   cm.
    Includes bibliographical references.
    ISBN-13: 978–0–313–34962–1 (alk. paper)
    1. Jesus Christ—Parables.   I. Title.
    BT375.3.C68   2008
    226.8′06–dc22   2007035406

British Library Cataloguing in Publication Data is available.

Library of Congress Catalog Card Number: 2007035406
ISBN-13: 978–0–313–34962–1

First published in 2008

Praeger Publishers, 88 Post Road West, Westport, CT 06881
An imprint of Greenwood Publishing Group, Inc.
www.praeger.com

Printed in the United States of America

The paper used in this book complies with the
Permanent Paper Standard issued by the National
Information Standards Organization (Z39.48–1984).

10 9 8 7 6 5 4 3 2 1

This book was written for the glory of God, who in his mercy,
called me to proclaim the gospel of Jesus Christ.

CONTENTS

ACKNOWLEDGMENTS

I wish to express deep appreciation to my family and parishioners, who have encouraged me to spread the teachings of Jesus Christ through my writings. I am particularly grateful to my wife Katherine and daughter Rebecca, who have assisted with this project. Also, special thanks to Lois Annechini for her computer and typing skills.

INTRODUCTION

Writing this book was a labor of love, for it's in the teachings of Jesus Christ that I find strength and hope. I have traveled far since I first accepted Jesus into my heart, but like most people, I continue to stumble, while seeking a more intimate relationship with God. There is a tendency to expect more of ourselves, especially when it comes to our Christianity, and I am no exception. Sometimes, however, we must claim victory over discouragement by looking back and realizing how far God's grace has brought us. Christianity is experiential and a matter of the heart. It is not perfection, but rather a developing journey that enables us to see ourselves in the light of God's Word and to prayerfully respond in a positive way. This is how one draws closer to the Lord and others.

The Scriptures provide us with guidelines and a road map. This is particularly true when we ponder the words of Christ, whose teachings pierce our hearts with transforming truth. While his words certainly convict us of our sins, they also speak of forgiveness, new beginnings, and eternal hope. During my years of theological training, I read numerous books which challenged my thinking and overall development. But, like a magnet, I continue to gravitate toward the teachings of Jesus. Only his words satisfy my hunger, fill life's void, and still the troubled waters.

My tenure as a state prison chaplain gave me invaluable insights into Jesus' teachings on love and forgiveness. On many occasions, including my experience with death row inmates and an execution, I witnessed penetrating examples of how the gospel of Christ reaches and transforms the darkest places in life. Although prison inmates experience intense struggle while trying to change their lives, God provides the door for forgiveness and spiritual freedom. Through the teachings and promises of Jesus, hearts of stone become flesh, with love replacing bitterness and anger. As the pastor for an execution, I was overwhelmed by the love of a man who was put to death. His faith and love for Christ was a witness to everyone present. His peaceful and moving manner challenged me to examine my faith and example. During the dark hours that led to his execution, he spoke about the ways in which the words of Christ changed his life, bringing forgiveness and certain hope in the midst of imminent death. His conversation alluded to the parables of Jesus, which reinforced for me the importance of these teachings in changing the hearts and lives of those who have been gripped by sin.

For me, the parables are pearls of divine grace that are experienced, not simply by reading them, but through continuous meditation and daily application. In other words, as we internalize our Lord's teachings, we walk in his truth, thus radiating a glow in a world darkened by sin. When Jesus speaks, our hearts are stirred, and as we continue to listen, an inner voice both changes and challenges us toward a new life. Love and forgiveness are no longer simply religious rhetoric but rather, realities. When we are free of pride and self-will, we begin to see the world through the eyes of our Creator. Regardless where we are in life, we become the living body of Jesus Christ. This sanctifying process brings glory to God through the building of his earthly kingdom. Our Savior's parables are not simply words to live by, but they change who we are. They set forth life's priorities and bring the inner transformation that enables God's grace to flow through our lives. This deepens our understanding and brings us into an intimate relationship with the Lord, which impacts upon all our relationships.

WHY SPEAK IN PARABLES?

Long before there were printing presses, copy machines, and computers, societies used storytelling techniques to convey beliefs, history, and traditions. This practice preceded the ministry of Jesus and continues today in many cultures. People are drawn to storytelling, which explains why many religious leaders employ this technique in their teaching. Jesus, however, was the master storyteller. Using familiar imagery found in nature and other recognizable sources, he engaged the people with lessons that confronted every aspect of their lives. It was a way to flesh out God's truth in a graphic and penetrating manner, thereby providing the tools for self-examination and change. His teachings are the seeds, which when internalized and nurtured, return us to the humanity God created us to be. The objective of these teachings is the freedom from self and the freedom to love.

Regardless of how much we resist, we find ourselves being drawn into our Savior's stories, either as a character in the plot or some aspect of creation. While the parables are simplistic in form and content, the reader must search for God's lessons. This process reveals one's desire to know the truth, while, at the same time, making it difficult to forget the lesson. When we labori ously seek to understand God's Word and how it applies to us, it becomes imprinted upon our hearts and minds. This serves as a constant reminder of God's expectations and will. Like "bugle calls," the parables awaken our igno rance and spiritual slumber, moving us toward repentance and a new life in Christ. These teachings were given for personal reflection, which means that they must be read slowly and prayerfully. As with all scripture, each time we read them, they will speak to us in new and challenging ways, while offering more enlightenment.

When studying these stories, there are some precautions to consider. For example, one must be careful not to dissect every word. The primary goal is to find the key message and central themes that have a personal applica tion. Also, be aware of the setting and circumstances in which Jesus told the story and how that translates into the present day. These are personal lessons; therefore, we must shed our pride and allow God to speak to us. Rather than understanding the parable as applying to someone else, the lessons are meant for each reader. This focused concentration is the vehicle through which we become one with Christ.

To provide for continuity of thought, this writing provides the text for each parable, with the explanation followed by probing questions for self-reflection. These questions, while serving as a meditative tool for spiritual development, may be used for devotional, as well as instructional and preaching purposes. The Scripture texts used in this publication are from the New International Version of the Bible, primarily because this translation is widely read and the result of over a hundred scholars working directly from the best Hebrew, Ara maic, and Greek sources. As stated in the Preface of the NIV Version, the participants were from the United States, Great Britain, Canada, Australia, and New Zealand. The denominations covered a broad spectrum, including Anglican, Assemblies of God, Baptist, Brethren, Christian Reformed, Church of Christ, Evangelical Free, Lutheran, Mennonite, Methodist, Nazarene, Pres byterian, Wesleyan, and other churches, all of which helped to safeguard the translation from sectarian bias. My use of the New International Version is not simply from an academic viewpoint, but also because it is easy to read and understand.[1]

The interpretations in this book are from a Protestant perspective of the parables. This is not to say that other Christian groups do not share the same understandings, nor does it mean that theologians and pastors within Protestant circles do not have some differences of opinion regarding certain texts, based upon their education and research. These factors were considered, with the result being a spiritual journey that hopefully benefits individuals from all spiritual persuasions.

One

THE SOWER

Text: Matthew 13:1–9; Mark 4:3–8; Luke 8:5–8 (NIV)

> That same day Jesus went out of the house and sat by the lake. Such large crowds gathered around him that he got into a boat and sat in it, while all the people stood on the shore. Then he told them many things in parables, saying: "A farmer went out to sow his seed. As he was scattering the seed, some fell along the path, and the birds came and ate it up. Some fell on rocky places, where it did not have much soil. It sprang up quickly, because the soil was shallow. But when the sun came up, the plants were scorched, and they withered because they had no root. Other seed fell among thorns, which grew up and choked the plants. Still other seed fell on good soil, where it produced a crop—a hundred, sixty or thirty times what was sown. He who has ears, let him hear."

In the twelfth chapter of Matthew, we find the Pharisees angry with Jesus and his apostles for their violation of the Sabbath laws. The Jewish Law, meticulously crafted by religious leaders, listed numerous prohibitions relating to Israel's holy day of rest. These man-made laws, which the leaders attributed to God, were overbearing on the people and impossible to interpret and follow. Even when Jesus healed someone on the Sabbath, the Pharisees accused him of breaking the work laws. They also accused Jesus of demonic activity when he healed a demon-possessed man on the Sabbath. In fact, any activity on the Sabbath was a violation that brought scrutiny. This may be difficult for us to comprehend in our liberal society, but it was a fact of life for the people of Jesus' day. There was always the fear of violating the law and the repercussions that might follow.

The leaders who continuously confronted Jesus certainly knew the letter of the Law, but they failed to comprehend God's mercy. Jesus' teachings of unconditional and universal love were foreign to their understanding of God's Word. Their legal minds could not grasp the concept of grace or God's inclusive love. But these leaders were not alone in their ignorance concerning spiritual matters, which included an openness to the gospel message. It was for this reason that Jesus challenged them with the *Parable of the Sower*. His listeners needed to know the obstacles that prevented them from hearing and internalizing God's message of forgiveness and reconciliation. Through his metaphorical use of nature, Jesus accomplished this in a most unique way. His listeners could relate to a sower in the field, for people lived off the land and were familiar with soil conditions and agricultural problems. This story was a graphic teaching that the Lord's listeners would not forget. Hopefully, the same truth applies to us today. What we find in this teaching are penetrating images that have a lasting impact upon the heart and mind.

Matthew tells us that a large crowd gathered around Jesus at a place along the Sea of Galilee, which forced him to escape to a nearby fishing boat pushed a short distance from the shore. This not only prevented him from being crushed by the gathering people, but it also enabled everyone present to see him and hear his words. It may have also thwarted some individuals from monopolizing his time, thus taking away from the urgency of his message. The serenity of the Sea of Galilee was a favorite place for Jesus, where he often mingled with the people to talk about God's kingdom. It was also a place where he often rested and spent time with his apostles for bonding and teaching purposes. There are certain environments that better enable us to hear God's voice, and this was one such location for Jesus and his disciples.

The *sower* in the parable represents anyone who spreads the good news of forgiveness and salvation through Jesus Christ. In this particular account, the sower is Jesus. However, as followers of Christ, we are commissioned to spread the seed of the gospel. As Christians, we are Jesus' living body, sharing in his ministry as kingdom builders. The *seed* is multifaceted, for it encompasses the many spiritual teachings aimed at inner transformation and spiritual growth found in the gospel message. The *soils* are the varied responses to God's call of mercy through Jesus Christ. In nature, the seed is dependent upon the condition and preparation of the soil. Likewise, receiving God's Word is dependent upon the condition and preparation of the human heart. The four specific soils in the parable are symbolic of the different responses to the gospel message. We need only examine our own lives to discover how the different soil conditions speak to us. At different times, we can find ourselves identifying with all four soils and how each one has influenced our spiritual sensitivity and lifestyle. This, of course, is the purpose of the parable, for it forces us to examine our inner life and relationship with God.

THE SEED ALONG THE PATH

The path through a farmer's field becomes very hard due to foot traffic. This situation makes it impossible for the seed to penetrate the soil. For the seed to germinate and bear results, the soil must first be prepared. This soil represents the stubborn heart. The sins of pride and self-will harden this heart, making it resistant to spiritual matters. Simply stated, people possessing this heart refuse to allow God into their lives. In some cases, these individuals even blame God for life's tragedies. Rather than honestly examining the condition of their heart, they look for other sources to blame for their difficulties and lack of grace. As a previous landscape contractor, I can attest to the problems resulting from hard soil. I recall spending many hours cultivating the soil on some properties prior to spreading seed. In certain situations, like the human heart, the soil refused to respond to my efforts. This resulted in the seed either being lost to the wind or providing food for the birds.

Jesus tells us that the birds came and ate the seed that fell on the hard path. Some biblical interpreters search for a deeper meaning in the verse, but it purely relates to a lost opportunity. What was available is now gone. This is a stark reminder that one day, when least expected, our opportunity to receive Christ will cease. In the parable, we learn that the seed was not wasted, implying that God's grace will always find a recipient.

There are people who spend their entire lives resisting God's grace and the movement of the Holy Spirit. In doing so, they lose the opportunities for purpose and personal fulfillment that the Lord makes available to them. We all know individuals who vehemently refuse to acknowledge God and his will for their lives. Others, however, wait in faith with an open heart, allowing the gospel seed to take root. Unfortunately, there are professing Christians who have not allowed Jesus Christ to change them, and this creates relational friction in church congregations. In our text, Jesus assures us that God's grace will always find a willing heart. The seed that is removed from one person will bring life to another. With some people, it simply takes a long time for the seed to germinate and bear fruit. In other words, hard hearts can be changed. It is important that we pray for the salvation of all people, beginning with our families. We often see our mission field as being outside the home, when those closest to us live in a state of hopelessness.

THE SEED ON ROCKY GROUND

Rocky ground lacks soil depth; therefore, whatever is planted will have a short life span. Not only is there insufficient soil for root growth, but the seed will not retain the moisture needed to sustain life. As a hiker, I have also become aware of these conditions. The next time you walk in the woods, take note of the changing soil conditions. In the rocky areas, you will find stunted or little plant growth. If you are a plant lover, you know that certain plants need to be placed in larger pots as they grow. When roots cannot find soil, their life expectancy is short. The results are similar for individuals who lack spiritual roots.

Soil on rocky ground represents the shallow heart. These are people who are initially enthusiastic about the gospel, but they lack staying power. They never develop the roots needed for spiritual health and growth. People with shallow hearts lack the commitment necessary to be rooted in their Christian walk, and this ultimately results in a separation from Christ and the Church. Numerous individuals, who at one time had a spiritual need, have fallen away from the Christian Church. This need is often found in baptism, weddings, sickness, or funerals. Catechism and counseling are other reasons why people seek out the Church. In many cases, it's simply a need for some type of service. But once the service is satisfied, the need for Christ and the Church comes to an end, that is, until another need arises.

As a pastor, I met many people who were first excited about a new lease on life made possible through Jesus Christ. However, it was not long before they disappeared from the church radarscope. Initial excitement does not always translate into the level of faith needed for a commitment. There is a tendency for people to revert back to their past lifestyles, and this is certainly true in spiritual matters. Jesus reminds us that many are called, but few remain committed. This was certainly true during our Savior's ministry. As long as Jesus was responding to personal desires, people remained at his side. This changed, however, when he was not what the people wanted him to be.

When the soil lacks depth, the sun will scorch and destroy what life there is. The searing sun can be compared to life's trials, which will unquestionably have a negative impact upon those who are not rooted in their faith. Such individuals are like a house without a foundation, trying to withstand a severe storm. To endure the difficulties of life, we must completely surrender our lives to God, trusting in his wisdom and sustaining grace. Whatever the loss or struggle, there must be a confidence in God's presence and compassion. The biblical story of Job is a prime example of faith in the midst of pain and loss. The apostles, particularly Paul, knew the importance of enduring as he encountered persecution.

THE SEED AMONG THE THORNS

Here is a powerful analogy taken straight from nature. Thorns, or weeds, are found everywhere, and in our garden, they choke out what we value and consider beautiful. As a homeowner, my least favorite job is pulling weeds. When nothing else seems to grow, the weeds show up everywhere, and weed killers only have temporary results. I once used a weed killer on my lawn and lost the majority of green plant life, revealing the high number of weeds lurking amidst the grass. Weeds even grow through a blacktop driveway, which seems impossible.

In our Christian life, weeds are symbolic of competing interests that choke out our spiritual growth, and they come in many forms. Actually, anything that substitutes for God can be a smothering weed. Today, our social calendars are so full that we find little time for the Lord. What should be the most important part of life becomes the least significant. Our suitcases are stuffed with many insignificant things, leaving no room for the God who seeks to save us from ourselves. We permit the material lures of the world to control our lives. Rather than being God's servants, we become slaves to secularism.

It is amazing how much time we spend working on our homes, and how little time is given to our spiritual temples. I am reminded of Jesus' visit to the home of Lazarus, where his sisters, Martha and Mary also resided. Jesus had an intimate relationship with the family and often visited them. On one such visit, we find Martha consumed with household chores and preparations for Jesus' stay, while Mary spent her time with Jesus listening to his words about the kingdom of God. In frustration, Martha came to Jesus and asked, "Lord, don't you care that my sister has left me to do the work by myself? Tell her to help me!" "Martha, Martha," the Lord answered, "you are worried and upset about many things, but only one thing is needed. Mary has chosen what is better, and it will not be taken from her" (Luke 10:38–42).

Jesus tells us not to worry about worldly things, for just as God takes care of nature, he will also provide for us. When our priority is God's kingdom and his righteousness, all that we need will be given to us (Matthew 6:25–34). This, of course, is a matter of faith, and here lies the stumbling block for many people. As small children have faith in their parents' care, we are called to have the same confidence in the Lord.

We must frequently examine our gardens and do the necessary weeding. How can we allow the beauty the Lord wishes to give us to be decimated by things that hold no eternal value? God is not warning us to give up hobbies and enjoyable entertainments, but he is telling us to set spiritual priorities and maintain a healthy balance. When life becomes an infested jungle full of competing interests, our spiritual soil is in peril. It is not unusual for pastors and other church leaders to be consumed by activities that have little or no spiritual value. Many times I have found myself neglecting my devotional life for parish-related work that had no nurturing value for anyone.

THE SEED THAT FALLS ON GOOD SOIL

Good Soil is the prepared and committed heart. It is an honest and humble heart open to God's words of truth and salvation. Regardless of trials, these individuals trust in God's will for their lives. The Scriptures provide many examples of the Lord's servants who, in spite of personal pain and loss, continued to trust in God. They knew that their hardships served a higher purpose. Mary, the mother of our Lord, is the ultimate example of this trust. When told by the angel Gabriel that she would miraculously conceive a child who would be called the Son of Most High, she was confused and troubled. Although this announcement was beyond human comprehension and would result in heartache and extreme loss, she surrendered her life to the Lord's will, saying, "I am the Lord's servant. May it be to me as you have said" (Luke 1:38). Little did Mary know, there was a painful path set before her, and her divine Son would echo her words of surrender prior to offering up his life for humanity's sins.

This committed heart bears eternal fruit for oneself, others, and for God. Sometimes we leave out ourselves, when in reality we are the first recipients of the grace that comes through our surrendered life. While the fruit we bear for God may not always be known to us, we are assured of its certainty within God's will. It's our prayerful submission to the Lord, along with personal gifts and opportunities, which determines whether we will produce a hundred, sixty, or thirty-fold. Although the initial step of surrender may be difficult, the longer we walk in the Spirit, the deeper our trust becomes.

REFLECTION

- Do pride and self-will ever harden your heart to God's call for a sacrificial life?

  We have all experienced those times when we knowingly resist the Lord's leading. Whenever our comfort zone is challenged, there is a tendency to allow pride and self-centeredness to control our thoughts and emotions. Rather than desiring to be partners with the Lord for a higher purpose, we oppose the inner voice and movement of the Holy Spirit.

- Do you have the spiritual depth that enables you to trust God in the midst of life's trials?

  It is one thing to trust God when everything is going well, yet another to have faith when the trials come our way. Many Christians simply lack the spiritual depth that is needed to walk in faith during life's trials. Instead of understanding challenges as a means to glorify the Lord, they respond in negative ways. Our spiritual journey must reflect the growth that comes through devotion, prayer, and worship. This means developing a spiritual life beyond the institutional Church and living the teachings of Christ every day.

- Are you allowing secular things to choke out God's grace and his will for your life?

  No one is removed from the ongoing influences of our secular society with all of its competing interests. We become overwhelmed with activities, entertainment, and projects that rob us of God's grace. Everyone must examine their lives in order to make the adjustments that allow the Lord into their daily living.

- From your life experiences, provide some examples of fruit-bearing soil.

  Bearing fruit for God can be understood in terms of our positive influence upon others, as well as how we have been blessed through the lives of Christians. It is amazing how fruit-bearing soil can change the direction of life for everyone involved.

Two

THE WHEAT AND TARES

Text: Matthew 13:24–30 (NIV)

> Jesus told them another parable: "The kingdom of heaven is like a man who sowed good seed in his field. But while everyone was sleeping, his enemy came and sowed weeds among the wheat, and went away. When the wheat sprouted and formed heads, then weeds also appeared. The owner's servants came to him and said, 'Sir, didn't you sow good seed in your field? Where then did the weeds come from?' 'An enemy did this,' he replied. The servants asked him, 'Do you want us to go and pull them up?' 'No,' he answered, 'because while you are pulling the weeds, you may root up the wheat with them. Let both grow together until the harvest. At that time I will tell the harvesters: First collect the weeds and tie them in bundles to be burned; then gather the wheat and bring it into my barn.'"

Jesus taught this parable along the Sea of Galilee, and this setting will not change for the following five parables. Considering that Jesus was in the same locale, one can assume that the circumstances are similar to those mentioned in *The Sower* introduction.

One encounters many similarities between *The Sower* and *The Wheat and Tares*, but rather than examining different soil types, Jesus now focuses upon a specific field containing good soil. In this same field, however, there are weeds growing along with the wheat. The owner, in response to his servants' concerns about the weeds, orders them to permit both wheat and weeds to grow together. Fearing that by pulling up the weeds, the wheat will also get uprooted, the owner tells his servants to wait. Later, during the harvest, the tares and wheat will be separated. Then, the harvesters will bundle up and burn the tares.

This parable primarily focuses upon the duality of good and evil in the world, using the wheat and the tares as a metaphor to illustrate this truth. It also describes God's final judgment, seen in the harvest gathering. God's judgment holds eternal realities for both the unrepentant and the righteous, with believers realizing joy and eternal bliss, while the unrighteous experience eternal despair and hopelessness.

In this lesson, the *sower* is the Son of Man; the *field* represents the world; and the *good seed* are Christ's followers who are commissioned to flourish and spread his message throughout the world. Jesus infers that the weeds symbolize the unrighteous, and as a result, the enemy that sows them is the devil. Satan has given birth to God's enemies, who seek to destroy the message of Jesus Christ. Also, note that the owner does not permit his servants to make judgments concerning the tares. Instead, he informs them that the final separation of the wheat from the tares will occur only during the Lord's Day of Harvest.

The parable presents several gnawing questions: Why is God allowing the tares and the wheat to grow together? In other words, why does God tolerate evil in the world? We understand that free will is an essential element of our humanity, without which we cannot freely love God and others. However, it also means that some people will find sinful ways to exercise and manipulate this freedom. So, in order to experience the free will which allows love, we often find ourselves confronted by evil. Since evil invades the fabric of our world, God's people must prayerfully find ways to confront it. First, we must understand temptations and the manifestation of sin within the context of personal need, and this speaks to the intercession of a Savior.

We live in a world where unrighteousness abounds. The power of sin is evident in every area of life, and it is easy to be drawn into a lifestyle that moves us away from God's grace. When we are not walking in the Spirit, we are in a weakened state and thus vulnerable to sinful influences. In his illustration of the *Vine and Branches*, Jesus warns us against separating ourselves from him. As the True Vine, we draw our strength and life from Christ (John 15:1–8). The discernment of evil and the power to resist temptation is only possible when we are rooted in our Savior's teachings. The apostle Paul emphasizes our need for the full armor of God. He wrote, "Put on the full armor of God so that you can take your stand against the devil's schemes" (Ephesians 6:11). In his letter to the Ephesians, Paul focuses upon the need to be rooted in truth, righteousness and faith. He also tells us to walk in the Spirit and to live a life of prayer (6:14–18). The full armor of God means a life that is totally given to the Lord. It is not enough to simply profess Christianity and allow ourselves to become complacent. Life involves decisions in the midst of spiritual warfare.

We must never underestimate the power of evil or assume that Christians are somehow removed from temptation. The Scriptures reveal that Jesus was tempted in every way possible, and his followers are not exempt. In his teachings, Jesus often spoke about evil and the power of temptation, emphasizing watchfulness and the need for constant prayer. Evil will be a reality until the Second Advent of Christ, when the harvest will take place and humanity will be judged.

Although this lesson paints an adverse picture, its final message is one of hope. In Jesus Christ, we have the power to both defeat the enemy and become a beacon of hope in a dark world. The story ends with the wheat and tares destined for eternal separation, and this should comfort us. Jesus' message tells us to stay the course and finish the race so that we might be among the wheat gathered into God's kingdom. Knowing the final outcome of this life and the eternal reality of the soul, we are encouraged to remain rooted in the one whose victory has already been established.

REFLECTION

• What tools does God provide to confront evil and temptation?

Although evil will always exist in our world, we are not only given the grace to stand firm, but to also strengthen our relationship with the Lord as we acknowledge his rule over all creation. Jesus confronted evil with God's Word and the promises found in the Scriptures. Unlike many people today, his strength was solely rooted in God's wisdom and power.

• How does the presence of evil impact the individual Christian and the mission of the Church?

The apostle Paul reminds us that our battle is against a foe whose presence is not always obvious. This may cause us to underestimate the presence of evil, thereby becoming a victim to its influences. Jesus told his disciples that they were to go out as sheep, but to be aware that they were amongst wolves who would seek to devour them.

• What is God's purpose in delaying Judgment Day?

Sometimes we forget that God's wisdom and knowledge cannot be known by us. Similarly, our perception of time is far different from a God who has no beginning or end. We do know, however, that it is the Lord's desire that no one perish under the penalty of sin. While this may be an impossibility, the continuing of this age and earthly existence will unquestionably bring an increase into God's kingdom.

Three

THE MUSTARD SEED

Text: Matthew 13:31, 32; Mark 4:31, 32; Luke 13:19 (NIV)

> He told them another parable: "The kingdom of heaven is like a mustard seed, which a man took and planted in his field. Though it is the smallest of all your seeds, yet when it grows, it is the largest of garden plants and becomes a tree, so that the birds of the air come and perch in its branches."

With *The Mustard Seed*, we continue Jesus' teachings along the Sea of Galilee. Talking about God's kingdom was the center of our Lord's discourses, and he often approached the subject in figurative ways, using powerful imagery to enhance his messages. As the Creator, he loved to wield nature metaphors to make his points, which helped his listeners view nature and their spirituality from new perspectives.

The mustard seed could be found in abundance throughout Palestine, both in wild and cultivated states. The mustard plant grows to a very large size along the Jordan River's banks. In comparison with other garden herbs, the mustard plant grows to the height of a small tree. While the seed is one of the smallest in nature, nothing can stop its rapid growth. Jesus used the mustard seed to communicate a powerful message about the kingdom of God. He tells us that, like the mustard seed, God's kingdom on earth began small, with little recognition from the world. But analogous to the mustard seed's vitality, God's message of hope endured and spread throughout the world. The kingdom that began with twelve students and the invisible movement of the Holy Spirit, has become God's unshakeable movement on earth. The catalyst and essence of this growth is found in God's love, which is manifested in the life, teachings, and sacrifice of Jesus.

Over the centuries, people have marveled over the enduring power of the gospel and the growth of the Church. When I think about the Church's inception, the following images come to mind: the seed of a woman; the birth of Jesus in a stable; an angelic announcement to shepherds working in a field; the call given to twelve common men to be followers and itinerant preachers; the movement of God's unseen Spirit; and crucifixion rather than coronation. These images, combined with the Church's continuous persecution, would make one think that failure was inevitable. History has seen the demise of many worldly kingdoms built upon military power and force, which have all crumbled into dust. But God's kingdom builds its foundation upon love, and no force can destroy it. Ours is an eternal kingdom where peace rules, where victory swallows up death. This kingdom begins in the heart of every person who receives Jesus Christ as Lord and Savior. Like the mustard seed plant, as people continue to receive the seed of the gospel, the kingdom will continue to expand in strength and size. This recycling process will continue until our Savior's return. To have mustard seed faith is not to be understood as having a small amount of trust in the Lord. Instead, it is to have a rapidly increasing faith that can be realized in one's own life, while serving as a witness to others. Jesus never taught that we were to be followers of little faith. His teachings, which call us to complete surrender, reveal the opposite.

REFLECTION

- How does this parable apply to your life?
  Areas you may wish to examine include:
  - Personal encouragement and development
  - God's sustaining grace and power
  - Hope and victory
  - Worldly position and recognition
  - Power against evil and temptation
  - Discipleship and the Church's mission.

  When pondering the above questions, it is important to realize that our personal faith in Jesus Christ is the catalyst that brings life to both individuals and the mission of the Church. It is faith that opens the door to God's kingdom and brings about its rapid growth. Additionally, it is personal faith that builds our lives into the image of Christ.

Four

THE LEAVEN

Text: Matthew 13:33; Luke 13:21 (NIV)

> He told them still another parable: "The kingdom of heaven is like yeast that a woman took and mixed into a large amount of flour until it worked all through the dough."

According to Matthew's text, the setting remained along the Sea of Galilee, and Jesus continued teaching with illustrations of God's kingdom, all of which were meant to provide spiritual insight into a particular aspect of God's rule. This lesson focuses upon the penetrating effect of the gospel; how the message of Jesus Christ permeated the hearts and lives of people all over the earth, bringing renewed life.

Leaven, such as yeast, is an additive used in batters and dough to cause them to rise during baking—its influence works to enliven the whole. In early times, people made leaven from fine white bran and kneaded it with unfermented or fermenting fruit juice, or with the meal of certain plants. Later, leaven was made from bread flour, kneaded without salt, and kept until it passed into a state of fermentation. Mosaic Law strictly forbade the use of leaven for priestly rituals, signifying that the offering was to be pure and without additives.

When Jesus used leaven as the focus of this lesson, he knew that everyone would be familiar with its use as an essential baking product. Again, we find our Savior using things that his listeners were familiar with to illustrate his teachings. At another place in the Scripture, Jesus referred to leaven when speaking about the Pharisees. Jesus accused them of being inflated with pride and ego, rather than assuming the role of humble servants as God commanded (Matthew 16:5–12).

The Leaven can be understood in both a personal and a universal context. Like the preceding parables, Jesus focuses on the mystery surrounding how God's kingdom is being built on earth. With this in mind, we must conclude that the *large amount of dough* represents the world and humanity, while the *leaven* is the Spirit of God, who has come into the world to change the lives of people. Like leaven changes and improves the quality of the baking process, we are continuously being changed into the image of Jesus Christ. The Israelites witnessed divine manifestations of power, such as plagues brought upon Egypt and the opening of the Red Sea, but it was Jesus who promised the indwelling presence of the Holy Spirit to bring spiritual life to the people. On the Day of Pentecost, God's holy leaven came as a mighty rushing wind, penetrating the hearts and lives of those, who in faith, would receive the gospel message. Although we cannot understand the essence or movement of the Spirit, we have witnessed the results in our lives and throughout the world.

Each person who receives Jesus into their life experiences the power of spiritual regeneration, changing their understanding and view of life. They develop a sensitivity and compassion toward others that previously was limited. Their new lives bring meaning and purpose, enabling them to see beyond themselves. Beginning to see life as one people, they share in the love and mission of Christ. As such, their presence in the world leads others to God's saving grace, thus bringing glory to the Creator of all life.

Through the intercessory work of Jesus Christ, the spreading of the gospel and the Holy Spirit's movement, people's lives continued to be changed as the kingdom is mysteriously built. We, who have been reconciled with God, have been given the ministry of reconciliation to proclaim to others. As the body of Christ on earth, we are empowered with divine leaven of the Holy Spirit, sharing in the work of Jesus as kingdom builders and awaiting the day when all of God's promises will be fulfilled. In the meantime, we continue to pray that God's kingdom will continue to increase. Christians are called by God to penetrate the world with the gospel message. As the salt of the earth, we are to bring our Savior's purifying love and power into the world. This is accomplished through faith, obedience, and the movement of the Holy Spirit. The gospel message touches the lives of countless people throughout the world, penetrating the darkest corners of society. I experienced this in the state prison system, where God's message of forgiveness and reconciliation transform the lives of many inmates.

REFLECTION

- How has the Holy Spirit changed your life?

  When the Holy Spirit enters our life, we become witnesses of his presence. Although we are still sinners, we become aware of an inner cleansing and transformation. This change brings a new perception and understanding of life. When we think about the many ways in which our lives have changed, we cannot help but give thanks to the Lord.

- Like the leaven in the parable, are you building up the kingdom of God? If so, what part are you playing?

  As God's leaven, we are kingdom builders by the Christ-like nature that we communicate. Our gifts and circumstances may vary, but we are one in purpose. We should give thought to the ways that God is using us for his glory, comparing our past life to the one we now live in the Spirit.

- What is the present and future understanding of this parable's lesson?

  This lesson is a message of power and hope, for it speaks to the personal and collective growth of God's kingdom. Unlike worldly kingdoms that are limited in scope and endurance, and often built upon violence, God's kingdom is built upon love and is eternal.

Five

THE HIDDEN TREASURE AND THE PEARL OF GREAT PRICE

Text: Matthew 13:44–46 (NIV)

"The kingdom of heaven is like treasure hidden in a field. When a man found it, he hid it again, and then in his joy went and sold all he had and bought the field. Again, the kingdom of heaven is like a merchant looking for fine pearls. When he found one of great value, he went away and sold everything he had and bought it."

Just prior to these two lessons on the kingdom, it appears that Jesus left the crowd and entered a house. If this is true, then these two parables were taught only to the disciples. They were important lessons for the apostles, who left everything behind to follow Jesus. No longer did they have the security of a home and a steady means of employment. They stepped out in faith to follow this mysterious man, who seemed to have the answers concerning life and death. But this does not suggest that they were without doubt. Over time, however, they became certain of the life that they had to follow. They walked away from their past, knowing the value of their life in Jesus Christ. They knew that he held the keys to life and death, and nothing was going to destroy their faith and commitment. Walking in the footsteps of Jesus brought meaning and purpose to their lives.

In life we make choices and set priorities, both of which influence the path that we will travel. Most of our time is given to secular activities, which we determine to be important, and we spend little time nourishing the soul. But, what is more important than our salvation, spiritual development, and God's plan for our lives? Is there a possession or achievement that can compare to

God's promises? If we know that nothing is more important than our relationship with God, then why is it so difficult to change our priorities? There are no easy answers to these questions because many factors, including societal norms, culture, desires, and philosophy of life, are involved. These issues also relate to our pride and self-will. We seldom contemplate leaving this world or think that the present directly affects the afterlife. To contemplate our death and how our present life speaks to this transition is not an easy topic for many people to discuss. We find it easier and more pleasant to remove such thoughts from our minds. But if life is eternal, then we must give thought to our eternal future and how we should be making preparation.

Jesus teaches us that our heart determines what is important to us. While society emphasizes the importance of achievement and material possessions to bring personal fulfillment, Jesus speaks about the eternal state of the soul. Unlike the body, which will return to the earth, the soul lives forever. This truth should move us to examine our lives, particularly the amount of time that we give to the Lord in prayer, worship, and our service to others.

I once asked a teenage Sunday-school class what they would give to live in a perfect environment. I described a place full of love that met all of their needs. Their expressions indicated a yearning for such a place, and without exception, each one agreed that they would give up everything, even their prized possessions. What astonished me was their response when I told them that this place was God's eternal kingdom. Even though they came from Christian families, I discovered that their thoughts were almost completely on worldly things. If adults were presented with this question, what would their response be? I doubt that it would be any different from this teenage class. Although the maturing process should bring increased understanding and wisdom, few people are living in the light of God's Word and promises. During my early years in ministry, I was naïve in believing that the Church was providing its members with the educational depth that led to spiritual maturity. While there are always exceptions, I found that the institutional church was not carrying out its mission. I also discovered that when such education was offered, few people took advantage of the opportunity.

These two parables share the same central theme, which is the eternal value of a life given to God. Jesus is both the hidden treasure and the pearl of great value that we must seek and cling to in faith and commitment. Like the characters in our Lord's allegory, we must be ready to make the necessary sacrifices in order to receive the gift of eternal life. God gave us his most precious gift, the life of his only begotten Son. It is this kind of personal sacrifice that we must be willing to give. We are to offer ourselves up as living sacrifices, serving God and one another.

When the man found the treasure in the field, what did he do? With joy, he sold all that he possessed and purchased the field. Further, to ensure that the gift would not be taken from him, he hid it again. He desperately wanted to keep the treasure, which he knew had great value. This lesson speaks to the essence of life, challenging us to determine what holds the most value in our lives. If our response is our relationship with God and our eternal future, then a prayerful self-examination is needed. Jesus reminds us that the cost of discipleship is a surrendered life (Matthew 10:32–39).

In the second parable, the merchant looked for a pearl of great value. Willing to pay any price, the man sold everything to possess the pearl because he knew it was priceless and could not be duplicated. Jesus tells us that the man searched for the pearl, and this is an important point. Even though the gospel is preached worldwide, Christ's message is distorted by secular influences and prevailing evil. Jesus assures us, however, that our search will not be in vain.

Sometimes, we need to ask ourselves what we are willing to give for the priceless gift of salvation. It is unfortunate that so many people keep God at a distance, only seeking him when difficulties arise. These individuals find the need for a Savior in time of trouble, but they do not want God to rule their daily lives. There are only two paths set before us, and even though we know this, countless people choose the road leading away from God's mercy. Although difficult to understand, it is a reality that will continue until Jesus returns. We are given every opportunity to know God, yet people continue to place their value in inanimate objects and what the world offers. So many people cast aside God's most valuable gift for things which have no eternal value.

REFLECTION

• What are you willing to give for your salvation?

> This may seem to be a difficult or ambiguous question, but it is a valid one. If you were asked to denounce your faith or meet violent results, what would be your response? In a society where there is freedom of religion, we may not be faced with this situation. But this question remains, for we are continuously asked to compromise our faith through life situations.

• How much time do you give to the Lord each day?

> Time given to the Lord is normally viewed in the context of prayer, devotional study, and congregational life. What are some other ways that you spend time with God? In your answer, list the benefits that you derive from this time.

- How would your family and friends describe your priorities?

  Everyone seems to have opinions about the lives of other people, much of which is distorted. While the Lord does not want us to judge others, it is important that we communicate priorities and a lifestyle that reveals the things of Jesus Christ. What do you find when you honestly look at your life?

- Are you willing to honestly examine your life and set priorities that are pleasing to God?

  This question directly relates to our desire to change those things in our life that are displeasing to the Lord. Are we willing to change some things, to the exclusion of others? Why is it difficult to address certain aspects of our lives?

Six

THE DRAG NET

Text: Matthew 13:47–50 (NIV)

> "Once again, the kingdom of heaven is like a net that was let down into the lake and caught all kinds of fish. When it was full, the fishermen pulled it up on the shore. Then they sat down and collected the good fish in baskets, but threw the bad away. This is how it will be at the end of the age. The angels will come and separate the wicked from the righteous and throw them into the fiery furnace, where there will be weeping and gnashing of teeth."

This is the last parable in Matthew's mini series of our Savior's teachings. Like the previous two lessons, it was probably told only to his disciples in a house along the Sea of Galilee. If so, it is likely the same residence that is recorded in Matthew 13:1.

The Drag Net is full of powerful symbolism that was familiar to our Lord's listeners. Fishing was a main source of livelihood and diet, and Jesus used the imagery of commercial fishing to address God's final judgment, when the righteous will be separated from the unrepentant. The certainty of the judgment speaks to our accountability before God and humanity. We are reminded that our life is a gift to be used for God's glory, and our responsibility is universal. At the judgment, everyone will stand before God to give an account of what they did with the opportunities that were offered them.

One must understand the following symbolism in order to provide further clarification of the lesson:

The Net: Jesus employs the imagery of the fishing net to paint a picture of God's final judgment, when all the peoples and nations will gather before

the throne of Jesus Christ to give an account of their lives. Like a fishing net
that gathers all species of fish, the Lord will bring humanity together on the
last day.

The Sea: He compares the sea to the wide expanse of the world, from which the
people will be gathered. God's spiritual net will gather them from the four
corners of the earth.

Fish of Every Kind: God's final judgment will include people from all genera-
tions, cultures, nationalities, and race. The people of the earth that are separated today will not be separated at the judgment.

The Angels: The angels are given the responsibility of separating the wicked from
the righteous. As in the past, they intervene in human affairs at God's bid-
ding.

Fiery Furnace: Eternal judgment is often described as flames, primarily because
fire brings thoughts of extreme pain and death. Like fire, nothing is more
painful than eternal separation from God's love and protection.

Weeping and Gnashing of Teeth: These words describe the response of those who
will be cast away from God's presence. In this life, they had their warnings
and opportunities, but they refused to listen.

The Scriptures give little detail about God's final judgment, but Jesus and
his apostles provide painful imagery through their teachings. Jesus' parable of
Lazarus and the Rich Man paints a graphic picture of the unrepentant soul
at death. This parable, along with other New Testament teachings, reveals a
separation between the faithful and the unrepentant. This separation casts the
unrighteous outside of God's presence. According to Jesus, the final abode of
the wicked will be an eternal state of outer darkness, void of the light generated
by God's presence. The righteous, however, will forever live in the presence of
their God and Savior in a place of perfect peace and joy.

In May of 1995, after serving over six years as a state prison chaplain, my
presence was requested at the execution of a death row inmate. Even though
they told me that the inmate desired my presence, I had no idea what to expect. Attending executions was part of my ministry, but only when the pris-
oner made the request.

The seven hours I spent with this individual will forever be etched in my
mind. The inmate was a professing Christian who was totally at peace with
God and spiritually prepared to leave this life. What was a sad and traumatic
experience became one of deep spiritual significance for both of us. Rather
than simply being his pastor for the remaining hours of his life, we bonded
through our shared faith and hope in Jesus Christ. We prayed together and
spoke about mutual struggles, as well as times of joy in our lives. I could not
believe that I would soon accompany him into the room where he would be

put to death. His faith in Christ truly changed him! Possessing the assurance of his salvation, he told me that he would soon be with his Savior, who had forgiven him and set him free. He emphasized that it was far better to be with Jesus than to serve the remainder of his life in prison.

Shortly after ten o'clock that evening, I walked alongside his gurney and said my last prayer on his behalf. The legal system judged and sentenced this young man, but through grace, he was a child of God and set free from his past life. I experienced firsthand how God's love reaches the darkest corners of life with the power to transform the worst sinners. While this parable warns us of God's judgment, it is a message of comfort and hope for those who come to the Lord through repentance and faith. My friend found solace in both God's promises and how his Savior could identify with his pain and execution.

Knowing that we are accountable before God should lead us to seek his forgiveness and grace while there is time. Here lies the central truth in this parable. In his love, Jesus repeatedly warns us about the realities of life and death, and this teaching is a clear example. Today is the day of preparation as we await the end of this age and the return of Christ. Yes, one day the net will be cast, and the angels will go forth to separate the wicked from the righteous. It is tragic to think that so many people will face their eternal destiny having chosen to live without God. Jesus told his disciples that they must work while there is daylight, meaning that one day their ministry will end, and the door to God's kingdom will close. Leading people to the grace that saves them from themselves and ultimately, the day of God's judgment, is our mission as Jesus' servants. Although we speak about God's judgment, the truth is that we bring judgment upon ourselves through the life that we choose. God, in his mercy, relentlessly tries to save us from the wrath to come, but his pleas so often fall upon deaf ears. As our heavenly parent, the Lord calls us into his safety and eternal rest, but few people respond.

REFLECTION

- Are you living in the light of Christ's teachings and divine accountability?

  Every person is accountable for the gift of life given to them. Christians are either beacons of light in a dark world, leading people to Jesus Christ, or they live in a manner that damages the gospel and the work of the Church.

- If the final judgment were today, would you be found amongst the righteous?

  The teachings of Jesus manifest an urgency, which speaks to every aspect of our life. To live in Christ is to be prepared to stand before him on the final day. While perfection is not possible in this life, we can have a pure heart that continuously strives after holiness.

• What can you do to better prepare for the Second Coming of Christ?

This is a personal inquiry that each person should examine. Although preparation addresses our inner life, it also extends to the needs around us.

Seven

THE UNMERCIFUL SERVANT

Text: Matthew 18:21–35 (NIV)

Then Peter came to Jesus and asked, "Lord, how many times shall I forgive my brother when he sins against me? Up to seven times?" Jesus answered, "I tell you, not seven times, but seventy-seven times. Therefore, the kingdom of heaven is like a king who wanted to settle accounts with his servants. As he began the settlement, a man who owed him ten thousand talents was brought to him. Since he was not able to pay, the master ordered that he and his wife and his children and all that he had be sold to repay the debt. The servant fell on his knees before him. 'Be patient with me,' he begged, 'and I will pay back everything.' The servant's master took pity on him, canceled the debt, and let him go. But when the servant went out, he found one of his fellow servants who owed him a hundred denarii. He grabbed him and began to choke him. 'Pay back what you owe me!' he demanded. His fellow servant fell to his knees and begged him, 'Be patient with me, and I will pay you back.' But he refused. Instead, he went off and had the man thrown into prison until he could pay the debt. When the other servants saw what had happened, they were greatly distressed and went and told their master everything that had happened. Then the master called the servant in. 'You wicked servant,' he said, 'I canceled all that debt of yours because you begged me to. Shouldn't you have had mercy on your fellow servant just as I had on you?' In anger his master turned him over to the jailers to be tortured, until he should pay back all he owed. This is how my heavenly Father will treat each of you unless you forgive your brother from your heart."

According to Matthew, this parable follows other teachings given by Jesus while he was in Capernaum with his disciples. Jesus told this story in response to Peter's question about forgiveness. Peter asked Jesus how many times he should forgive someone who sins against him. Before Jesus could respond to the question, Peter suggested that forgiving someone up to seven times seemed more than sufficient. The answer that Jesus gave Peter was seventy times seven, meaning that forgiveness has no conditions or limits. This unquestionably shocked Peter, who thought that he had a generous heart.

The first-century Jewish rabbis taught that a person was to forgive another up to three times but not the fourth. Peter, who more than doubled the legal guidelines, found himself confronted with a new, radical teaching. Jesus tells us that forgiving others is not a suggestion but rather a divine mandate. In his teachings, our Savior emphasizes the link between a forgiving heart and our salvation. The apostles' writings reiterate this truth, including the apostle Paul who tells us that we must forgive others, just as God in Christ forgives us. The Lord's Prayer makes no distinction between friends and enemies. Instead, it is a promise that we will forgive others regardless of their offense.

Forgiveness is not a natural response toward those who violate us. As you know, our immediate reaction to provocation is rarely one of understanding toward the person. Both the desire and ability to forgive is a gift of the Spirit that comes through persistent prayer. Even mature Christians struggle with forgiveness, and without prayer, an open door to pride and bitterness remains. However, even though we struggle with our feelings, the Lord honors sincere prayer.

We may not forget an offence, but it is crucial that we not harbor or nurture animosity and revenge. Over the years, I prayed for individuals whom I believe thought ill of me. My petitions not only included the other person, but also my attitude toward them. We tend to leave ourselves out of such prayers, thereby blocking the healing power of the Spirit.

Having been both a police officer and prison chaplain, I was in the midst of the criminal element, interacting with individuals who committed heinous crimes. Serving as a chaplain in the state prison system especially challenged me. It is one thing to arrest a criminal and yet another to be their pastor. My chaplaincy was obviously a test of my Christian love for society's outcasts, but through prayer I developed a compassion that I thought was impossible to possess. Although there were struggles, the Holy Spirit continued to remind me that Jesus sacrificed his life for all sinners, and that God seeks the lost wherever they may be found. The prison system is a vast mission field often neglected by the Church.

When we approach God with a humble and contrite heart, he assures us of his healing grace. Prayer, however, does not replace the need for verbal exchange in difficult relationships. Approaching others in love may facilitate healing and reconciliation. If not, it may at least release the tension and conflict in a relationship. Only when we prayerfully confront our negative feelings can we truly love all people, including those whom we perceive to be our enemies. Our goal is to fill our hearts with the love of Calvary, where Jesus sought the Father's forgiveness for his enemies. This is the love that brings inner peace and sets us free from the bondage of anger and bitterness.

The Lord's teaching describes a servant unable to pay a debt that he owed his master. The man found himself in a hopeless state, and in his frustration and pain he begged the master to allot him more time. Then, in a surprising story twist, the master expresses an abundance of compassion. Rather than give the servant an extension, he completely cancels the debt.

Now, having received such mercy, the servant should have been sensitive toward others in the same situation, but this was not the case. Instead, when a fellow servant was indebted to him, he showed no mercy. He immediately had the man thrown into prison until the debt was paid. The parable concludes the way it should. When the other servants told the master what happened, he turned the thankless servant over to the jailers. Jesus tells us that everyone who fails to forgive faces this plight. Rather than mere lip service, forgiveness calls for a change of heart toward the person.

This lesson impacts everyone, including those who claim to walk in the footsteps of Jesus. How many people, in their pride and lack of spiritual maturity, truly forgive those who offend them? Maybe, we should ask the question in another way. How many people desire to forgive others? These questions directly speak to our relationship with God, for we cannot forgive others if Christ's love is not moving us.

Numerous professing Christians harbor animosity toward others. In their judgment, they are somehow justified for their attitudes and actions. I encountered church leaders who even refused to speak to family members during Christian fellowships. These people regularly attend church but never internalized the gospel message. Jesus was always amazed how people, especially religious leaders, could miss the meaning of God's Word.

When we, in humility and repentance, cry out to our Master for forgiveness, he is quick to reveal his mercy. Therefore, how can we refuse to give others this same spirit of understanding and love? To believe that God will forgive us when we refuse to extend the same mercy to others is to reject our Savior's teachings. Our journey with God is not simply one of increasing knowledge, but also an increase in love for *all* people. To harbor anger or resentment toward any person is to lose the inner peace given by the Holy Spirit. Only when we are at peace with God and all people can we possess the joy of salvation. I cannot imagine walking through life without God's peace and joy, but this is the reality with many individuals, including active church members. Rather than waiting upon the other person, forgiveness is a process that begins with our prayers.

REFLECTION

• What is your definition of forgiveness?

Forgiveness is an inner cleansing that removes the bitterness and anger from a person's heart. While forgetting another person's sins may not be possible, God can remove the animosity.

• How does forgiveness benefit both us and other people?

A forgiving heart is one that shares in the nature and work of Christ. Only forgiveness brings us into a relationship with God and one another.

• Explain how forgiveness is understood within the context of the Church's mission?

Salvation does not exist apart from forgiveness. This is the essence of the gospel and the reason why Jesus sacrificially gave his life.

Eight

THE LABORERS IN THE VINEYARD

Text: Matthew 20:1–16 (NIV)

"For the kingdom of heaven is like a landowner who went out early in the morning to hire men to work in his vineyard. He agreed to pay them a denarius for the day and sent them into his vineyard. About the third hour he went out and saw others standing in the marketplace doing nothing. He told them, 'You also go and work in my vineyard, and I will pay you whatever is right.' So they went. He went out again about the sixth hour and the ninth hour and did the same thing. About the eleventh hour he went out and found still others standing around. He asked them, 'Why have you been standing here all day long doing nothing?' 'Because no one has hired us,' they answered. He said to them, 'You also go and work in my vineyard.' When evening came, the owner of the vineyard said to his foreman, 'Call the workers and pay them their wages, beginning with the last ones hired and going on to the first.' The workers who were hired about the eleventh hour came and each received a denarius. So when those came who were hired first, they expected to receive more. But each one of them also received a denarius. When they received it, they began to grumble against the landowner. 'These men who were hired last worked only one hour,' they said, 'and you have made them equal to us who have borne the burden of the work and the heat of the day.' But he answered one of them, 'Friend, I am not being unfair to you. Didn't you agree to work for a denarius? Take your pay and go. I want to give the man who was hired last the same as I gave you. Don't I have the right to do what I want with my own money? Or are you envious because I am generous?' So, the last will be first, and the first will be last."

In this lesson, Jesus focuses upon the sins of jealousy and resentment. Although it was directed at a Jewish audience, particularly the Pharisees and the scribes, it is a message for everyone. The Jews misunderstood their role as God's chosen people. Rather than seeing themselves as examples and teachers of God's Word for those outside their spiritual circle, many of them developed a superior attitude toward others, especially non-Jews. The Israelites were given the Law, patriarchs, and the prophets. The Lord promised Abraham a great nation led by divine providence. God's intervention released the Jews from Egyptian slavery and, through military victories, brought them into the Promised Land. God spoke to the Jews, and gave them places for worship and learning. Thinking of Gentiles coming into God's kingdom without being raised in Judaism caused jealousy, resentment, and anger among the Jewish leaders. Even if God accepted the Gentiles into his kingdom, how could they receive the same benefits as the Jews, who served God since the days of the patriarchs?

Misconceptions concerning the kingdom were many, stemming from years of spiritual ignorance, distorted teachings, and national pride. Such problems and issues were even prevalent amongst the apostles. The apostle Paul, who taught that Gentiles need not pass through Judaism to become Christians, was often at odds with the other apostles and leaders. As teachers laying down the foundation for Christianity, this parable would especially be helpful for these spiritual leaders.

In this lesson, Jesus describes a landowner who seeks out workers for his vineyard. On four separate occasions, he went out looking for laborers. He told the first workers hired that they would each receive a denarius for a day's work. Those hired later would accept what the landowner deemed reasonable compensation. When evening came, the landowner told his foreman to pay the workers. A reversal of the norm, the foreman began with the last people hired. Now, what we find next is also unusual. Those hired last, working only one hour, were paid the same amount as the laborers who worked all day in the intense heart. Needless to say, it did not take long before the first hired started grumbling about this perceived injustice.

In response to the mounting complaints, the landowner asked the laborers who worked all day if he shortchanged them. After all, they agreed to work all day for one denarius. The property owner then told them that he had the right to do what he desired with his money, and he suggested that they were simply envious of his generosity. The parable concludes with Jesus saying to his disciples, "The last will be first and the first will be last." This statement is similar to the one found in Matthew 19:30 when Jesus responded to Peter's concerns about worldly security.

The contradictions in this story, although intentionally employed by Jesus, make this parable more difficult to understand than Jesus' other teachings on the kingdom. In a spiritual sense, we know that the *landowner* is God the Father, the *foreman* is Jesus, and the *vineyard* represents the building of God's kingdom on earth. The *workers*, of course, are the people who respond to the Father's call. Keeping this symbolism in mind aids our comprehension of this message.

Just as the landowner left his property to search for willing workers, God in Christ left his realm of glory to call us to serve his kingdom. But, instead of receiving a monetary reward, our gift is salvation, which comes through faith rather than works. Like the workers in the vineyard, God's reward is the same for everyone, regardless when they enter the kingdom, which demonstrates our equality in Christ.

This lesson shows how the landowner repeatedly searched the marketplace for new workers to fill his vineyard. Likewise, through the gospel message and movement of the Holy Spirit, God continuously reaches out to those who are spiritually idle, inviting them into his vineyard. It is indeed interesting that those who worked only one hour were paid first. Reversing the payment order allowed all the workers to know the other's wage. If the landowner paid them in hiring order, the first hired would have left the vineyard satisfied with their single denarius. Their complaints surfaced when they compared their wages with the workers hired later. Skillfully, Jesus used this story to spotlight the sinful attitudes that surface when we compare ourselves with other people. In this case, resentment and anger emerged amongst the workers.

Comparing ourselves with others often makes us judgmental, and this destroys our ability to love. The parable reminds us that God is the only judge, which gives him the right to dispense grace in the manner he desires. Maintaining unity within a congregation is one of the greatest challenges for any pastor. People are always concerned about the lifestyles, actions, and failings of fellow Christians. Rather than concentrating upon their own spiritual needs and development, they see themselves as superior. This attitude is sometimes seen among established church members, who resent the suggestions and involvement of new members. While church tenure should benefit the life of a congregation, it is often used in a manipulative and destructive manner. We tend to forget that Christianity is a welcome mat and gateway for all people.

Years ago I pastored a church that experienced rapid growth. Within a matter of three years, the attendance doubled, bringing people into our fellowship from all walks of life. Many of these families had no church background, and they were unaware of the expectations that certain individuals were placing on them. It was not long before some people began voicing their concerns about the lifestyles of particular people. There were even complaints that some of the new children were a negative influence on our youngsters. Some of these matters obviously needed to be examined, and as I spent time with these families, I began to hear voices of jealousy from longstanding members in the congregation. This intensified when some of the new people wanted to become actively involved in the church. Jealousy is alive and well in our churches, especially toward new folks. Christians often forget that Jesus gave his life for all people, and the mission of the Church is to receive and nurture all who seek forgiveness and salvation. Whenever we think about giving up on others, we must remember that God never gives up on us. Somehow it is easy to see the flaws in someone else's life, while failing to recognize our own sins and past lifestyles.

The last verse in this parable is confusing because it is the antithesis of secular thinking. In what way are the first last and the last first? How does this statement fit into the teaching? What appears to be a disconnected afterthought is actually a truth fundamental to our Christianity. In a succinct way, Jesus emphasizes that humility is the Lord's will, and people who envision themselves as superior are least worthy in God's eyes. Although the world praises and applauds individuals for their positions of power and deeds, the Lord honors humility. In fact, God abhors any form of self-glorification. Jesus' statement can also be understood within the context of equality, meaning that regardless of our past life, worldly accomplishments or church standing, we are all one and equal in Jesus Christ. In other words, no one is superior in God's mind.

Regardless how long we work in God's vineyard, the reward remains the same because salvation cannot be earned or quantified. It is a free gift that begins with a repentant heart. We must never compare what God has given to us with the good he gives to others. Our goal is simply to walk the humble path of our Savior, allowing the sanctifying work of the Holy Spirit to bring us into a closer relationship with God and his mission on earth. It is imperative that we focus upon our own lives, while making every effort to walk in our Savior's teachings.

REFLECTION

• What is our role in God's kingdom? As a worker in God's vineyard, what is our primary concern?

> The work of the kingdom is to bring people to the saving grace of Jesus Christ. No one is excluded from God's love, and disciples are to be both witnesses and communicators of the gospel. This necessitates that we exemplify the life of Jesus

in all that we do. Our Savior came to us as a humble servant, and we are to follow the same path. The atonement of Christ speaks to the equality of all people, a truth that must be a primary concern.

- What does it mean to be content with what the Lord has given us, and why is it important for one's spiritual development?

  Contentment is both a state of mind and an attitude of the heart. It is real-ized through serving the Lord and knowing that all gifts are heavenly sent. A contented person is one who acknowledges God's sovereignty and trusts in his wisdom and power. Such people live with thankful hearts, realizing the void and hopelessness that exist apart from divine grace. Those who walk in this light experience continuous spiritual development.

Nine

THE TWO SONS

Text: Matthew 21:28–32 (NIV)

"What do you think? There was a man who had two sons. He went to the first and said, 'Son, go and work today in the vineyard.' 'I will not,' he answered, but later he changed his mind and went. Then the father went to the other son and said the same thing. He answered, 'I will, sir,' but he did not go. Which of the two did what his father wanted?" "The first," they answered. Jesus said to them, "I tell you the truth, the tax collectors and the prostitutes are entering the kingdom of God ahead of you. For John came to you to show you the way of righteousness, and you did not believe him, but the tax collectors and the prostitutes did. And even after you saw this, you did not repent and believe him."

The passages preceding this text set the stage for our parable. In his anger, Jesus entered the temple in Jerusalem and turned over the money changers and the tables of those selling doves. God's house of prayer became a marketplace for profit, and the religious leaders promoted this activity. This hypocrisy of the Pharisees, Sadducees, and scribes was a continuous bone of contention with Jesus, and he never hesitated to address it in his preaching and teaching of God's kingdom. Jesus knew that many of the religious leaders were a detriment to the spiritual lives of the people. The Lord's intention that they be servants and examples of true holiness resulted in superior attitudes. Although they held religious offices, they were not willing to allow God to change their lives. Whatever promises they made before the Lord were broken for a life of self-glorification.

The morning following the temple incident, Jesus and his disciples walked back to the city. Feeling hunger, Jesus approached a fig tree and found nothing on the tree but leaves. He commanded that the tree never bear fruit again, and immediately the tree withered. Jesus' interaction with the fig tree became a lesson on Israel's unproductiveness and God's judgment, which undoubtedly shocked the disciples. We next find Jesus entering the temple where the chief priests and elders questioned his authority. Since he held no religious or political office, they wanted to know what right he had to preach and challenge the established order. Then, Jesus asked them a question about John the Baptist, who preached repentance for the forgiveness of sins. Knowing that they rejected John's ministry, Jesus aimed this question directly at these chief priests and elders. Since they refused to respond to Jesus, he remained mute and never answered their question concerning his authority. Instead, he told them this parable.

Jesus frequently admonished the religious leaders for their lip service and manipulation of the Law. His rebukes centered upon their lack of humility and love. Rather than being teachers and servants of God, they separated themselves from the people, seeking special favors and praise. The parable Jesus chose to share with them addresses individuals who claim obedience to God, but they only serve themselves. Like the second son in the story, even though he made a promise and appears to be obedient, there is no change of heart. This hypocrisy and deception exists within all religious circles, extending beyond church leaders. It is a cancer that distorts and tarnishes the message, example, and mission of the Church.

The key points in our Lord's teaching relate to broken promises, hypocrisy, and spiritual deception. The Pharisees and other religious leaders were supposed to serve God, but their self-righteous attitudes resulted in broken promises and a false spirituality. Jesus reminded these men of John's call to repentance, but their pride proved an obstacle to a changed life.

In the parable, Jesus asks us a question. Is it better to make a promise to God and break it, or say no to God and later have a change of heart? Many sinners, who once rejected God, are entering the kingdom through repentance and faith, while the self-righteous, who refuse to acknowledge their sins, remain lost in their pride. The second son in this story changed his mind and received the gift of life.

In his book, *The Parables He Told*, David Redding provides some penetrating insights into the sinful nature. He writes:

> A man no sooner makes up his mind to follow God than he is besieged by the
> temptation merely to flatter Him instead. So the temple has always been filled

with suitably dressed, legally acceptable, and superficially loyal imposters . . . The hypocrite can take over the pulpit, monopolize the pew, drown out others with his hymns and prayers. He never forgets to say "Amen" at the right time and with just the right inflection . . . He makes a few good-looking sacrifices to get away without having to make "the sacrifice of God . . . a broken and a contrite heart." His faith is crystallized. It is a tomb in which he is burying himself.[1]

In conclusion, things are not always what they appear in the Church of Jesus Christ. We need a continuous and honest self-examination of our lives that allows the Holy Spirit to bring us into a deeper relationship with God. Many people have a difficult time examining their hearts and actions in the light of our Lord's teachings. Rather than acknowledge their sins, they find it easier to shift blame and judge others. This refusal to honestly look at themselves and prayerfully seek God's forgiveness and transforming power is the reason why many professing Christians struggle in their spiritual walk. The lessons and sermons are always applied to someone else, and even when personal conviction occurs, it is resisted. Few individuals are open to the pain that accompanies self-examination and repentance, as well as the discipline required for spiritual development.

The complaint of non-Christians is the hypocrisy that is prevalent in the Church. This is reinforced as people become more aware of the crimes committed by church leaders. We all know that professing a lifestyle does not mean that one is living it. The damage that is done through hypocrisy and deceit is incomprehensible, for it recycles from one generation to another. The result is not only anger but also mistrust of those who profess to be spiritual guides. Pastors are always cognizant of the example that they are communicating inside the church, as well as in the community and within their own family. In fact, it is not unusual for someone to remind them of their faults. In the prison system, I was always aware that inmates were observing me to determine if I could be trusted as their pastor. Some prison chaplains develop institutional attitudes over a period of time. They lose the love of Christ, which prevents them from being a servant.

Jesus emphatically states that many who claim discipleship have not kept their promises to God, and yet, some of the worst sinners who initially rejected God, have repented and turned their lives around. Using examples of tax collectors and prostitutes finding salvation, Jesus directed this parable to the Jewish leaders, whose pride and self-righteousness kept them from reaching out to the lost segments of society.

In a lesson about bearing spiritual fruit, Jesus said: "Not everyone who says to me, 'Lord, Lord,' will enter the kingdom of heaven, but only he who does the will of my Father who is in heaven. Many will say to me on that day, 'Lord, Lord, did we not prophesy in your name, and in your name drive out demons and perform many miracles?' Then I will tell them plainly, 'I never knew you. Away from me, you evildoers!'" (Matthew 7:21–23).

We must be careful not to fall victim in believing that affiliation with Christ and the Church translates into a salvation relationship. Instead, we should prayerfully seek a deeper walk with God in which we ask for the gifts that continuously transform us into the image of Jesus Christ. Spiritual life is a process that always strives for the heart and mind of the Savior.

In Jesus' teaching on the *Wise and Foolish Builders*, he said, "Everyone who hears these words of mine and does not put them into practice is like a foolish man who built his house on sand. The rain came down, the streams rose, and the winds blew and beat against the house, and it fell with a great crash" (Matthew 7:26, 27). As in all of the Savior's teachings, this parable applies to everyone. While refusing to look at ourselves, we have the tendency to judge others. We made promises to God through baptism, catechism, church membership, and marriage, but have we kept these promises? We also promised to follow the teachings of Jesus, which includes forgiving and loving all people. Needless to say, many people considered to be hopeless sinners by some are entering God's kingdom, while numerous church members and leaders remain lost in their refusal to repent and walk in the Spirit. When I received Christ into my life, my focus was the teachings found in the New Testament. Although I acknowledge the inspiration of the Hebrew Bible with its many lessons and spiritual insights, it was the teachings of Jesus and the apostles that spoke to my deepest needs. While I am cognizant of my sins and infirmities, I know that in Christ, hypocrisy can be replaced with humility and love. This teaching reminds us of the spiritual goals that are set before us.

REFLECTION

• Have you made promises to God that have been broken?
  The following areas may help you in your response:

  Church membership and worship
  Personal devotions and prayer
  Infant and/or adult baptism
  Catechism class
  Tithing
  Spiritual development, with an emphasis upon love and forgiveness toward all
      people

We should frequently take time to reflect upon the promises we have made to God. During times of personal need, we often offer up promises to the Lord, sometimes knowing in advance that they will not be kept. In other instances, our intentions may be good, but we lack the spiritual fortitude necessary for endurance and commitment. Even in our worldly interactions, we tend to be people of broken promises, which has its destructive effects.

- Do you ever question the authority of Jesus Christ?

  Christians are quick to claim the authority of Jesus Christ, until that authority conflicts with their personal desires and plans. Most people want a Savior who will provide sustaining grace and bring them into God's eternal kingdom, but they struggle with having a Savior who will be the Lord over their life. Everyone has some degree of difficulty with authority, the roots of which are found in early childhood. What exists in our secular life is also found in our relationship with the Lord.

- Are you spiritually productive for God? If so, in what way?

  Spiritual productivity takes many forms, all of which need to be examined. For example, how much of our day is spent with God, and what is the quality of that time? Is Christ at the center of all that we do? In other words, are his teachings considered in our daily activities? Also, do we pray for God's leading and then patiently wait upon the Lord? Finally, what more can we do to be spiritually productive?

- How much time do you spend examining your inner life?

  Few people give serious thought to their inner life. What was emphasized by the mystics and early Church fathers has fallen along the path of time. We are action people who get things done, often to our own demise. The Lord calls us to journey within ourselves, connecting with our thoughts, emotions, and the echoes of our soul. As you do this, you may be surprised with what you find.

- Are you ever guilty of pride and hypocrisy? If so, how should you confront these sinful attitudes?

  Who can claim to be free of all pride and hypocrisy? While this may sound like a defeatist response, it emphasizes the need for spiritual maturity. As we become more Christ-like, the sins of pride and hypocrisy begin to dissipate. Keep in mind, however, that Christian maturity develops from a life that is completely surrendered to the Lord. As the apostle Paul wrote, we are to offer up our lives as living sacrifices unto the Lord. All sin can be kept in check through the indwelling power of the Holy Spirit, who both convicts and leads us to the fount of forgiveness, cleansing, and renewal.

• What characteristics should a Christian possess?

> All we need to do is ponder the life and teachings of Jesus, and we will immediately realize the characteristics that God wants us to possess. These are found in the gifts of the Holy Spirit and can be summarized with the word *love*. They are the gifts that bring inner transformation, enabling us to be servants of God and a priesthood of believers.

Ten

THE TENANTS

Text: Matthew 21:33–46; Mark 12:1–12; Luke 20:9–19 (NIV)

"Listen to another parable: There was a landowner who planted a vineyard. He put a wall around it, dug a winepress in it and built a watchtower. Then he rented the vineyard to some farmers and went away on a journey. When the harvest time approached, he sent his servants to the tenants to collect his fruit. The tenants seized his servants; they beat one, killed another, and stoned a third. Then he sent other servants to them, more than the first time, and the tenants treated them the same way. Last of all, he sent his son to them. 'They will respect my son,' he said. But when the tenants saw the son, they said to each other, 'This is the heir. Come, let's kill him and take his inheritance.' So they took him and threw him out of the vineyard and killed him. Therefore, when the owner of the vineyard comes, what will he do to those tenants?" "He will bring those wretches to a wretched end," they replied, "and he will rent the vineyard to other tenants, who will give him his share of the crop at harvest time." Jesus said to them, "Have you never read in the Scriptures: 'The stone the builders rejected has become the capstone; the Lord has done this and it is marvelous in our eyes.' Therefore I tell you that the kingdom of God will be taken away from you and given to people who will produce its fruit. He who falls on this stone will be broken to pieces, but he on whom it falls will be crushed." When the chief priests and the Pharisees heard Jesus' parables, they knew he was talking about them. They looked for a way to arrest him, but they were afraid of the crowd because the people held that he was a prophet.

The setting and circumstances of this parable remain the same as the previous teaching. Jesus is again confronting the hypocrisy of the Jewish leaders, but this passage also focuses upon the leaders' rejection of Jesus as the Anointed One sent by God. Although Jesus does not clearly proclaim to be the Messiah, he forces his listeners to ponder the possibility. But, like those sent by God before him, they see Jesus as a threat to their authority and power and plan to assassinate him before he becomes too popular. If the people followed Jesus, their leadership positions would not only be challenged by the masses, but they also would be questioned by Roman authorities.

Matthew tells us that the chief priests and Pharisees understood that Jesus was talking about them. They also knew that Jesus had a large following, for many of the people believed he was a prophet. However, this was not going to thwart their plot to eliminate him. Instead of examining the Scriptures in light of Jesus' teachings and claims, they completely rejected his message. The rejection of Christ as the prophesied Messiah began with the ministry of John the Baptist, who came to prepare the way for Jesus. Their rejection of John's preaching directly impacted their responses to the gospel.

This lesson has a universal and timeless application because people of every generation refuse to consider the teachings and divinity of Christ. Even church members question the absolute authority of Jesus over their lives. The Church has gone through many changes over the centuries, with some of the most recent ones being quite significant, for they have challenged orthodox Christian beliefs and influenced the direction of denominations. Rather than churches thought of as simply being liberal or conservative, there are congregations that lack the essential beliefs of the Church. But what has become evident are the tensions surrounding certain issues, such as the inspiration of scripture and sexual orientation. A number of churches have left their roots over these differences. What is disturbing are the movements that seek to destroy the teachings and claims of Jesus Christ. It is not uncommon for some seminaries to question the gospel message, and even our Savior's resurrection. These individuals and groups judge the Scriptures, rather than allowing the Scriptures to judge them. They discredit the words of Christ that do not fit into their agenda. There is little difference in what is going on today, as opposed to the rejection of Jesus' authority during his earthly ministry. With these considerations in mind, let us examine the lesson set forth in the parable. Insight into the following terms will provide a foundation for our understanding

THE LANDOWNER

As the life force of creation, we acknowledge the sovereignty and providence of God. The Lord is the master and judge of all that he created. He is the potter, and we are the clay in his hands to be molded according to his will. As the landowner, God justifiably has expectations for those he created.

THE VINEYARD

If you research the word *vineyard*, you will find its many uses in the Bible. There are Mosaic regulations relating to eating the fruit of the vineyard during the first three years of its planting. During the fourth year, the fruit is holy to the Lord. Only in the fifth year does the vines' produce fall entirely to the owner's disposal (Leviticus 19:23–25). Everyone who listened to this parable possessed knowledge of vineyards and understood how they were metaphorically used in Judaism. Jesus simply took imagery already known to the people and applied his own creative touch. The spiritual use of vineyards can be found in other teachings, including those discussed in this book.

The vine was a national symbol of Israel. It is written that Israel was a vine brought out of Egypt (Psalms 80:8; Isaiah 5:2). To dwell under the vine and fig tree was an emblem of domestic happiness and peace (I Kings 4:25; Psalms 128:3; Micah 4:4). To plant vineyards and eat the fruit was a figure of peaceful prosperity (Nehemiah 9:25; Isaiah 65:21; Ezekiel 28:26), and the rapid growth of the vine symbolically suggested the growth of the saints in grace (Hosea 14:7). However, the rebellious people of Israel are compared to *wild grapes* and an *empty vine*. In such cases, the vineyard represents a figure of Israel's chastisement for sin (Isaiah 5:7; 27:2; Jeremiah 12:10), and the failure of the vineyard symbolized severe calamities (Isaiah 32:10). In his teachings, Jesus used vine imagery to represent the spiritual union existing between him and believers, with unfruitful branches being mere professors of faith and discipleship (John 15:1–6). He emphasizes that he is the True Vine, and whoever breaks away from him will experience spiritual death (John 15:1–6).

In this text, the vineyard represents the Jewish nation with its advantages and opportunities. Being people blessed by God and set apart for divine service, the Jews were given the responsibility that the Church has today, but their leaders often rejected the preaching and warnings of the patriarchs and prophets. As indicated in the parable, God's prophetic servants were frequently the victims of violence for their messages that called for repentance and spiritual transformation. History reveals that people have always rejected God's Word, even those who claim to be believers.

The vineyard is the world to which Jesus came, where he taught the people, preached the gospel, and sacrificed his life. It's also where Jesus commissioned the Church to carry on his work and where the Holy Spirit seeks out the lost.

We reside in God's great vineyard, and he calls us to spiritual separation and participation in the ministry of reconciliation. Every person who confesses Jesus as Lord is given the mantle of discipleship, proclaiming him through example, the Word and compassionate acts.

THE TENANTS

Although this reference can be applied in a broader scenario, Jesus metaphorically described the tenants as Israel's leaders, who God placed in positions of trust to teach and lead the people into holiness. But, rather than living according to God's commands found in Scripture and the voice of the prophets, they developed a system of works that excluded the people they were called to serve. Unlike Jesus, who came to us as a humble servant, they placed themselves above the people. The Hebrew Bible records the mistreatment of God's messengers. Circumstances are different today, but violence toward God's servants continues throughout the world. Instead of adhering to the spiritual principles of understanding and tolerance, the differences between people often take the path of conflict. Not only is this found between those professing different religions, but it is also present between those who share the same doctrinal beliefs.

THE LANDOWNER'S SON

The landowner's son is Jesus, and the reference to the son being killed by the tenants is a prophecy of the crucifixion, which was planned by the Jewish leaders and carried out by the Roman government. Instead of listening to the Son and considering his teachings and claims, Israel's leaders acted with scorn and retribution. No one could confront them, not even the owner's Son. Hearts infected with pride and self-will are closed to divine truth.

Have you wondered how Jesus would be received today if he walked our streets with the same message and announcement of his divinity? I doubt that things would be different, for the human heart has not changed. Even after two thousand years, responses to the Savior remain the same. Regardless of our increased knowledge and understanding about spiritual matters, sinful desires and lifestyles remain an obstacle to the Spirit's movement. As Jesus said, "Many are invited, but few are chosen" (Matthew 22:14).

God placed us in a position of trust, and we are accountable to him. He called us to be servants and fruit bearers for the kingdom. When Jesus returns in all his glory, he will judge everyone according to their spiritual depth, gifts, and opportunities. As Christ tarries, we must carry on his work, realizing that opportunities are temporary. Jesus is the capstone of the Church, and to reject his message and mission is to reject the Father who sent him. God initiated our salvation by sending us his Son, but we can only receive him through faith. But the concept of faith is a stumbling block for many who believe that salvation is earned through works. This secular thinking, which was evident in many of Israel's leaders, remains prevalent today. Our minds are tuned into a work ethic which often clouds our reasoning and spiritual sensitivity. In fact, there is a sense of pride as we engage in certain activities and accomplishments. For many people, the concept of salvation through faith is an irrational abstraction.

Jesus told the Jews that the kingdom would be taken away from them and given to a people who would bear fruit. While some construe this as a pronouncement of Israel's eternal damnation, it should be interpreted on an individual level. Whether Gentile or Jew, our response to Jesus Christ is a personal matter. The judgment of other people lies within the wisdom and sovereignty of God. One's salvation is a matter of the heart, the state of which is only known by the Lord.

This lesson also has special significance for the Church, both individually and collectively. While the owner of the vineyard is away, Christians must produce a harvest. We do this in love, knowing that our labor is not in vain, because in due time it will bear fruit. As God's tenants, we have the responsibility of inviting others into his vineyard so that they might receive the Spirit's fruit and find eternal life.

REFLECTION

- As God's tenants, what is our responsibility?

    We are the caretakers of all that belongs to God. Whether human life, nature, or animal life, God commands that our decisions are aligned with his will in accordance with the Scriptures. Christians are also proclaimers of the gospel through word and example. Central to this is that of being a peacemaker and channel for God's grace.

- What is your motivation for working in the vineyard?

    There is nothing in this life that has more value and has more personal fulfillment than being a servant of the Lord. There are many roads in life, but the only one built upon divine love is the path of Jesus Christ. Discipleship provides answers to life and satisfies our deepest needs. True blessings come through service to God and one another.

- Jesus tells us that he is the Capstone, and those who fall on him will be crushed. Explain this statement.

  This is a graphic expression telling us that rejecting Jesus as Lord and Savior thwarts divine grace and leads us away from God's kingdom. Jesus is the way to the Father, and to knowingly reject him results in eternal death.

- In what ways do people today harm God's messengers?

  Depending where one resides in the world, attacks upon Christian workers vary. In our culture, negative responses to the gospel are normally subtle. This, however, does not mean that aggression is not possible. What we typically find is a disinterest that may cause people to distance themselves from us. Our material world also plays a part in one's negative response to the gospel. Unless confronted with a personal emergency, people simply find no need for God in their lives.

Eleven

THE WEDDING BANQUET

Text: Matthew 22:1–14 (NIV)

> Jesus spoke to them again in parables, saying: "The kingdom of heaven is like a king who prepared a wedding banquet for his son. He sent his servants to those who had been invited to the banquet to tell them to come, but they refused to come. Then he sent some more servants and said, 'Tell those who have been invited that I have prepared my dinner: My oxen and fattened cattle have been butchered, and everything is ready. Come to the wedding banquet.' But they paid no attention and went off—one to his field, another to his business. The rest seized his servants, mistreated them and killed them. The king was enraged. He sent his army and destroyed those murderers and burned their city. Then he said to his servants, 'The wedding banquet is ready, but those I invited did not deserve to come. Go to the street corners and invite to the banquet anyone you find.' So the servants went out into the streets and gathered all the people they could find, both good and bad, and the wedding hall was filled with guests. But when the king came in to see the guests, he noticed a man there who was not wearing wedding clothes. 'Friend,' he asked, 'how did you get in here without wedding clothes?' The man was speechless. Then the king told the attendants, 'Tie him hand and foot, and throw him outside, into the darkness, where there will be weeping and gnashing of teeth,' For many are invited, but few are chosen."

Like many of Jesus' parables, this lesson addresses the theme of rejecting God and the resulting judgment people bring upon themselves. It is the story of those who refuse God's grace: of people caught up in the world and themselves. These individuals give little thought to matters of the soul and how they will spend eternity. While they may know what is best for them, they insist upon following a destructive path. The longer they resist God, the harder their heart becomes. Sometimes, they even develop an antagonism toward Christ and the Church. As a pastor, I have been the recipient of those who are angry at God. I especially encounter this with non-Christians while officiating at funerals. Those who are suffering often project their guilt and anger at God's representatives. Instead of clinging to the promise of grace and eternal life, they find avenues for their frustration, pain, and their lack of faith.

Jesus also brings attention to imposters, who deceptively wear the cloak of spirituality but never surrendered their hearts to God. People can display a spiritual exterior, but whitewashing the pump does not make the water pure. All imposters are a detriment to the Christian example and the Church's mission. Their false lives distort God's Word and reinforce the negative thoughts and feelings of individuals who look upon the Church with suspicion. The world observes the lives of Christians to see if they live what they profess. From the day that we experience the life of Jesus, family members, friends, and even strangers look for the changes that should accompany our new life. As previously stated, I experienced this in the prison system, where inmates tested my claim to love and forgive all people.

Jesus compares the kingdom of heaven to a king who prepared a wedding banquet for his son and sent out invitations to the festivities. In this story, the banquet is symbolic of the salvation celebration given for those who respond to the gospel invitation offered through Jesus Christ. The *son* is Jesus, the eternal bridegroom of the faithful. Found in this parable and other teachings, Jesus uses the marriage analogy to clarify his relationship with us. This metaphor needs little explanation because we know what makes a good marriage and how we must strive to improve the marriage relationship. Just as secular marriage is rooted in faith, love, and commitment, these same ingredients bond our marriage to Christ.

The *servants* mentioned in the story are those whom God commissioned over the centuries to proclaim his Word and issue divine warnings to the people. These servants include the patriarchs, prophets, and particular leaders of Israel, who set before the people a holy path to follow. In the New Testament era, they were the apostles, and today, God's servants are the followers of Jesus Christ. The invitation offered by the Lord's servants will continue to go forth across the earth until Jesus returns. As God's ambassadors, we are stewards of his message of forgiveness and hope. This calling is accomplished through example, witness, and confession of faith.

Although scholars view the three distinct invitations differently, a general treatment will serve us better. Jesus intended to give a simple historical overview to reveal the responses to God's continuous call for repentance and a changed life. God gave the first invitation to the Jews, who rejected the patriarchs' and prophets' warnings. Their sins met with devastating results, including captivity and exile into foreign lands. Beginning with a prophetic element, the second invitation began with the ministry of John the Baptist and continued with Jesus and the early Church. Although God included the Gentiles in this call, it was first given to the Jews, whose leadership refused to accept the gospel message.

The parable indicates that this lack of response led to a third invitation. The king told the servants to go into the streets and invite anyone who responded. Lifestyle was not an issue, but their desire to attend the banquet was important. As a result of this invitation, the banquet hall became full. The king accepted outcasts and hopeless sinners, both Jew and Gentile alike, into the joyous festivities. In contrast with the others who walked away from the opportunity, these individuals desired to attend and immediately responded to the call. Although their lives were not reflective of righteousness, their hearts were open to a change.

The high banquet attendance pleased the king, but he noticed a man not wearing the proper attire. As previously noted, this man was an imposter who tried to enter the celebration unnoticed. He apparently fooled the guests but could not deceive the king, who told the attendants to throw him outside into the darkness. There, the imposter would experience the weeping and gnashing of teeth. This graphic language unquestionably speaks to God's judgment at the end of the age.

Unfortunately, the Christian Church has its share of imposters, including clergy and people in high positions, who sometimes use the Church to satisfy their independence and worldly needs. In our lesson, the imposter's fate is the plight of all who refuse to receive God's mercy. Jesus wants us to know that today is the day of salvation, for we are not promised another minute of life. The Lord desires that we all receive the eternal joy awaiting us in his kingdom. In response to questions regarding the delay in Jesus' return, Peter said, "The Lord is not slow in keeping his promise, as some understand slowness. He is patient with you, not wanting anyone to perish, but everyone to come to repentance" (II Peter 3:9).

This parable describes an historical picture of a world that repeatedly refuses God's offer of forgiveness and salvation, who seek answers and fulfillment in other ways, including riches and pleasures. While these are gifts from God, they do not satisfy the void that only the Lord can fill.

But regardless of the countless people who refuse God's mercy and rule over their lives, others will respond and fill the banquet hall, entering a place of perfect harmony where God meets every need. Those who have entered the Lord's banquet hall are people from all over the earth. As the parable points out, they are individuals whose past lives were marred by sin. Jesus makes it clear that he came as a physician for the spiritually sick and dying. This is the love and power of God's message of reconciliation.

REFLECTION

- How should God's universal and inclusive invitation address our attitudes toward others?

    We all are the Lord's children; therefore, there are no limits or bounds when it comes to God's love and offer of salvation. Our ethnocentric attitudes sometimes categorize people and nations, believing that some people are below us. We tend to draw a circle around our lives, allowing some people in, to the exclusion of others. Those who have traveled to other countries realize that regardless of culture and religion, we are one humanity and equally loved by God. Our attitude should be the same as that of Christ, remembering that he gave his life for every person.

- Is there a time limit on the Lord's invitation?

    The Scriptures teach that today is the day of salvation, meaning that one day all opportunities to receive Jesus Christ will end. We do not know the time of our death or when Jesus will return for the final judgment. It is imperative, therefore, that we be prepared.

- How do you understand the wedding banquet?

    The wedding banquet, whether understood literally or in symbolic terms, speaks to both the joy and celebration of entering God's eternal realm. There is a celebration for every person to whom Jesus Christ has given life. Just as we celebrate a natural birth, the heavens ring with joy over every spiritual birth that brings victory over sin or death.

- What does it mean to be a false disciple?

    A false disciple is one whose life does not reflect their profession. Rather than walking in the teachings and love of Christ, they have their roots in the things of the world. While they may enjoy the fellowship of the Church, they have not experienced an inner change.

Twelve

THE TEN VIRGINS

Text: Matthew 25:1–13 (NIV)

"At that time the kingdom of heaven will be like ten virgins who took their lamps and went out to meet the bridegroom. Five of them were foolish and five were wise. The foolish ones took their lamps but did not take any oil with them. The wise, however, took oil in jars along with their lamps. The bridegroom was a long time in coming, and they all became drowsy and fell asleep. At midnight the cry rang out: 'Here's the bridegroom! Come out to meet him!' Then all the virgins woke up and trimmed their lamps. The foolish ones said to the wise, 'Give us some of your oil; our lamps are going out.' 'No,' they replied, 'there may not be enough for both us and you. Instead, go to those who sell oil and buy some for yourselves.' But while they were on their way to buy the oil, the bridegroom arrived. The virgins who were ready went in with him to the wedding banquet. And the door was shut. Later the others also came. 'Sir! Sir!' they said. 'Open the door for us!' But he replied, 'I tell you the truth, I don't know you.' Therefore keep watch, because you do not know the day or the hour."

The passages that precede this lesson speak to the end of the age and the Second Coming of Jesus. The apostles often heard Jesus speak about this topic in figurative language, but on this occasion their curiosity and concern lead them to question him about the incidents leading up to this event. They wanted to know what will occur, and how they will know when the end is near. This discourse begins with Matthew 24:1 and continues through the chapter.

Prior to sharing this parable with his apostles, Jesus told them that only the Father knows the day and hour of his return. However, he does reveal that it will be sudden and when least expected. People will go about their normal routines until divine intervention suddenly changes the world. This will usher in both the final judgment and God's eternal kingdom. The apostle Paul tells us that the rapture of the living, along with those who already died in Christ, will commence, with the unrepentant left behind for judgment. To the Corinthians, Paul wrote, "I tell you a mystery: We will not all sleep, but we will all be changed—in a flash, in the twinkling of an eye, at the last trumpet. For the trumpet will sound, the dead will be raised imperishable, and we will be changed" (I Corinthians 15:51, 52). In writing to the Thessalonians, Paul said:

> For the Lord himself will come down from heaven, with a loud command, with the voice of the archangel and with the trumpet call of God, and the dead in Christ will rise first. After that, we who are still alive and are left will be caught up with them in the clouds to meet the Lord. And so we will be with the Lord forever. (I Thessalonians 4:16, 17)

The Ten Virgins warns us about things to come—one day life as we know it will end. Since the beginning of time, evil tainted the world, destroying countless lives, and the saints of all ages cry out to God for justice (Revelation 6:9–11). Evil abounds even in the Church, distorting God's Word and fracturing relationships and entire congregations. Few people follow the path of forgiveness and unconditional love, but God promises an end to iniquity. This will happen when Jesus returns as judge and ruler of all people. Meanwhile, we must remain vigilant, not allowing ourselves to become spiritually complacent or fall into disbelief. As in the past, what God promises, he will do. He charges us to remain patient in our faith and service. Each person is responsible for their own preparation, a daily process rooted in personal devotion and prayer. Although the Church is important to our spiritual growth, we must go beyond its limitations and imperfections by developing a personal relationship with the Lord. So many people rely only on the Sunday morning worship service to feed their soul. Although we need the grace, discipline, and fellowship of the Church, its ministry is limited in depth and scope. To grow in Christ and to remain strong in our faith requires daily interaction with God and his Word.

This lesson is prophetic of our Savior's Second Coming and the predicament many will experience when he returns—being unprepared! While our Lord's return will be a time of joy and victory for the faithful, the unrepentant will find themselves eternally separated from God's love and care. Free will allows us to make decisions and choose our life's path, and through this parable, Jesus encourages us to choose the path of faith and preparation. Life is but a fleeting moment, and its uncertainty adds to this lesson's crucial nature. Everyday, God gives us opportunities to examine our lives and make the necessary changes, but when Jesus returns, these opportunities will be gone. We must not put off the most important decision of our life, living for Christ and the Church. People tend to think that they have time, a belief particularly found in young adults who think that their youth affords them time to turn their lives around. Yet, whether we meet an untimely death or experience Christ's sudden return, more time is not guaranteed. Resulting from a hard heart, procrastination is a sin that robs countless people of salvation.

This parable's structure is interesting in that it reflects ancient Jewish wedding customs, a detail the Lord's listeners recognized. Unlike today, wedding banquets were spontaneous; therefore, it was important for everyone to be prepared for the wedding party's arrival, especially the bridegroom. Marriages typically took place at the home of the bride's parents and included a feast that sometimes lasted seven days. These celebrations were often elaborate events with guests wearing fancy attire and musicians supplying entertainment. As a part of the wedding ritual, the bridegroom went to the bride's house where she and her maidens anxiously awaited his arrival. The bridegroom never arranged a set time for his arrival, making the bride and her maidens test their patience and prepare for his entrance. Once he arrived, the bridegroom escorted the bride and the wedding party to his home or his father's home where festivities took place. The bridegroom's removal of the bride was the essence of the marriage ceremony. Afterward, the wedding party returned to the home of the bride's father where the rituals continued.[1]

This lesson symbolically identifies Jesus as the heavenly *bridegroom*, and the *ten virgins*, or maidens, as the professing Church waiting for his arrival. The burning *oil lamps* symbolize the faith and commitment of the righteous. Their hearts glow for Christ with a burning faith that witnesses to the world. The *wedding banquet*, as seen in other teachings, is a metaphor describing the celebration and joy of entering God's kingdom. This is a victory party for everyone who finishes the race. Like enduring a long and painful marathon, we cross the finish line to find a celebration that ushers in our eternal lives with the Lord. Victory will swallow up disease and death, and the only tears will be those of joy.

On the surface, the ten virgins had two things in common. They all possessed knowledge of the bridegroom and his impending arrival. However, when the unexpected occurs, the similarities end. No one ever thought the bridegroom would arrive at midnight! Because of this delay, five virgins ran out of oil. They simply failed to prepare! But how could this happen if they knew that the bridegroom would eventually arrive? Did they assume that they could prepare at the last minute? How could they not realize that they might need more oil? Regarding the return of Jesus, we could pose similar questions today. Although we have no information concerning the day and hour of his return, God promises that it will occur. So, why have so many people fallen into a spiritual slumber?

During my last years in full-time ministry, I engaged in many conversations with clergy regarding the state of the Church. Without exception, I was told of a diminishing interest on the part of congregations. Pastors informed me of the constant struggle to keep people excited about their life in Christ. Even the spiritual seasons, such as Lent, seem to have little significance to the present generation. Churches of different denominations often combine their worship services during Lent to help fill the pews. Clergy report a spiritual laziness and complacency on all levels of ministry. Some researchers who have studied this situation believe that the nature of our society, combined with weak pulpits and educational programs, have helped create this dilemma. The thriving churches are those that minister to people on many levels with biblical, yet practical messages that speak of daily living.

This parable focuses upon four interconnecting scriptural truths. First, our Lord's return is both certain and imminent. There is evidence of this found in Jesus' promise and the apostles' writings. Peter and John fill their epistles with this certain hope, and the apostle Paul even provides some specifics. Although the Hebrew Bible never addresses this topic, the Book of Job contains an interesting statement believed by some as prophetic. Job said, "I know that my Redeemer lives, and that in the end he will stand upon the earth" (Job 19:25). Many Christians have no idea of the many biblical passages that relate to the Second Advent of Christ. A topical Bible is a good starting point for studying this cosmic and life changing event promised by God.

The second truth speaks of the sudden and unexpected nature of Jesus' return. Jesus makes it clear that only the Father knows when this will happen. He tells us that neither he nor the angels in heaven possess this knowledge, but Jesus does mention that the event will be sudden and when least expected. His return will be like a flash of lightening across the sky, with no time to change one's destiny (Matthew 24:27). Like all intercessory events, Jesus' return is in accordance with God's will and timing. No biblical insight or human knowledge provides any clues. Some individuals have tried to place the Second Advent within a certain time frame, but they were wrong. Simply stated, we will never know this information until the event is upon us. What would happen if we were privy to this mystery? How would that impact humanity? Would prior knowledge really change the human heart and result in an enduring commitment to Christ and the Church? The fact is, we know that Jesus will return, and I doubt that a set calendar date will make any difference when it comes to a surrendered life. Those who seek to know and please God desire to serve him now. Actually, not knowing when Christ will return tests our heart's desire.

The need for preparation is the third key point found in the parable. The tragedy of life is not that it ends so quickly, but that we wait so long to begin it. Those who ignore their spiritual needs walk a dangerous path, because no one knows when death or divine intervention will bring all opportunities to an end. God continuously speaks to our hearts and sense of reasoning, but are we listening?

Finally, this teaching reminds us that faith and Christian character cannot be transferred from one person to another. As you read, the wise virgins refused to let the foolish borrow oil. We stand before God alone, with our state of readiness revealed before the Lord of the universe. I have met individuals who believe that Christian parents or friends will somehow be character references for them before God. Others think that church affiliation alone makes a difference on judgment day. Jesus, however, emphasizes that only a life surrendered in faith will save us. This parable clearly discloses that once the door to God's kingdom closes, no amount of pleading will change one's eternal future. For Jesus Christ to know us, we need a personal relationship with him.

REFLECTION

- How should we prepare for the Second Advent of Christ?

    Preparation for the Second Coming of Jesus Christ goes far beyond knowledge and attending worship services. As the parable states, we must be ready for the unexpected, and this necessitates living both in and for the gospel. Jesus spoke about lukewarm Christians, and how they were not worthy of the kingdom. He also taught that those who set their hands to the plow and look back, yearning the old life of sin, were also unworthy. In plain words, Jesus is either the center of our life, or he is not. Like the maidens in our story, we must not slumber, believing that we will have time to replenish our lamps.

- According to this parable, can a person lose their salvation?

    This parable, as well as Jesus' other teachings, emphatically state that we can fall from grace. Just as free will allows us to love God, it also provides a way to remove ourselves from his grace by falling back into sinful living. It is clear that our names can be removed from the Book of Life. Eternal security, which is believed by some Christians, is conditional upon the faith that we exercise through a surrendered life. The apostle Paul was clear on this topic when he said that salvation is not a one-time situation. Instead, it is a matter of faith from beginning to end. Anyone who becomes complacent, believing that they cannot lose their salvation, has fallen into Satan's trap.

• Why is it taking so long for Jesus to return?

The apostles believed that Jesus would return in their lifetime. This is one reason why there was a delay in writing the four Gospels. Over the years, both church leaders and lay people have tried to predict the Second Advent based upon current events, and they have all been wrong. It appears that people refuse to believe the teachings of Jesus, who emphasized that only the Father knows the day and hour of his return. This cosmic and life-changing event will never be known by humanity. As previously stated, the apostle Peter believed that the delay in our Lord's return means the salvation of more people. While this may be true, our concern is preparation—to remain strong in our faith until that day. This is the message of our teaching.

Thirteen

THE TALENTS

Text: Matthew 25:14–30 (NIV)

"Again it will be like a man going on a journey, who called his servants and entrusted his property to them. To one he gave five talents of money, to another two talents, and to another one talent, each according to his ability. Then he went on his journey. The man who had received the five talents went at once and put his money to work and gained five more. So, also, the one with the two talents gained two more. But the man who received the one talent went off, dug a hole in the ground and hid his master's money. After a long time the master of those servants returned and settled accounts with them. The man who received the five talents brought the other five. 'Master,' he said, 'you entrusted me with five talents. See, I have gained five more.' His master replied, 'Well done, good and faithful servant! You have been faithful with a few things; I will put you in charge of many things. Come and share you master's happiness!' The man with the two talents also came. 'Master,' he said, 'you entrusted me with two talents; see, I have two more.' His master replied, 'Well done, good and faithful servant! You have been faithful with a few things; I will put you in charge of many things. Come and share your master's happiness!' Then the man who had received one talent came. 'Master,' he said, 'I knew that you are hard man, harvesting where you have not sown and gathering where you have not scattered seed. So I was afraid and went out and hid your talent in the ground. See, here is what belongs to you.' His master replied, 'You wicked, lazy servant! So you knew that I harvest where I have not sown and gather where I have not scattered seed? Well then, you should have put my money on deposit with the bankers, so that when I returned I would have received it back with interest. Take the talent from him and give it to the one who has the ten talents. For everyone who has will be given more, and he will have an abundance. Whoever does not have, even what he has will be taken from him. And throw that worthless servant outside, into the darkness, where there will be weeping and gnashing of teeth.'"

This lesson continues the theme of preparedness by accentuating our God-given talents. Jesus reminds us that everything we have is a gift from God to be used for his glory. Although we all share similar gifts, the Lord endowed each of us with particular talents and opportunities. Many people, including Christians, refuse to believe they possess significant talents. While they may see others' gifts, they cannot recognize their own uniqueness. Sometimes we forget that our talents are like planted seeds that need to be nurtured and developed. It is prayer that sparks this growth process. When I studied for the ministry, I struggled with public speaking, obviously a concern for someone called to preach and teach God's Word. Only through faith and continuous prayer did these gifts begin to develop. The gift was already there, but it required divine intervention, education, and practical experience.

We often recognize our gifts in descriptive terms and as particular talents. While some people do possess conspicuous talents, we should consider our entire life as a gift to be offered up to God. Also, as we grow in Christ, gifts of the Spirit emerge. It is amazing how spiritual maturity manifests gifts that were once latent or even nonexistent. Regardless where we are in life or the extent of our education, the Lord gives us gifts that require constant development.

The apostle Paul reminds us that the greatest gift is unconditional love. This love is found in the sacrificial life of Jesus, who gave his life for his enemies and society's outcasts. Paul told the Corinthian Church that without love, we are nothing. He wrote that love is patient, kind, and not self-seeking. It is the only gift that never fails (I Corinthians 13). When we pray for the heart of Jesus, we seek to love all people. This divine gift also brings other talents to the surface. Those who grow in God's love find themselves assuming the characteristics of Jesus, which enables an understanding of life not previously realized. This opens new doors for personal development, thereby creating additional gifts that bring glory to God through our service.

Even though they may be unconscious, investments are a part of life. Whether it is a farmer investing in a crop or someone investing in the stock market, people seek beneficial increases. We make investments in our employment with the anticipation of future benefits, and we invest in our children's college education, hoping that it will have positive results for them after graduation. When you think about it, our thoughts and actions continuously focus upon some type of increase that brings fulfillment and improves life. Sometimes, we entrust others to invest for us, and this is what occurs in this parable. Our Creator entrusted us with talents to be invested for him, and after a certain time period the accountability factor comes into play. God wants us to feed upon the teachings and promises of Christ that transform us into servants, a priesthood of believers, who through love, help build his kingdom on earth. Everyone who receives the indwelling power of the Holy Spirit becomes a witness of God's presence in the world. In a sense, our entire life is a gift that is given to the humanity for which Jesus gave his life. There was nothing in the nature of our Savior that was self-serving, for his entire life was God's gift to us. This is the example that we are to emulate as we invest our lives for the Lord.

The currency used in the parable was the talent, the largest measure of weight the Jews had for precious metal. Its actual weight was somewhere between fifty-eight and ninety-three pounds, comprising at least 1,500 copper shekels. During the time of Christ, money was measured in weight rather than coin value, and the talent was considered the maximum weight a man could carry.[1] Seeing that the master used the *talent* for his investments, one may conclude that Jesus intentionally chose this large monetary amount because it relates to our value before God and his investment in us. We must never underestimate how valuable we are to the Lord and the many ways we can serve him throughout our lifetime. Sometimes, the smallest acts of kindness bring a person to Jesus Christ, and whatever we do in Christ's name will recycle through those touched by us. When looking back upon our life's journey, we become aware of individuals who touched us in special ways. Through our interactions with them, we experienced God's presence and leading. It may simply have been their words of encouragement that made a difference in our lives. There have been people in my life who unknowingly led me to the Lord and brought me to the place where I decided to enter the ministry. Although I may never see them again, they are always with me in spirit.

The parable speaks about a master who gathered his servants together, giving each one talents to invest for him before he left on a long journey. To one man, he gave five talents, to another, two, and to the third man, he gave one talent. When the master returned, he assembled the servants together to settle accounts. The first two servants did well, for they doubled their investments. Both the master and the servants were pleased with the increase, and because they did so well, the master increased their responsibilities. These men accomplished what the master asked, and he now trusted them with future investments.

However, the third servant chose a different course and refused to invest his single talent. When questioned by his master about his decision, this man responded by saying he believed his master was unreasonable and incapable of being satisfied, leading him to bury the talent. The master chastised him for his excuses and disobedience. After all, this servant was no different than the other two men, whose obedience resulted in a monetary increase. In fact, the master gave the third servant less responsibility than the other two workers. Angered by the third man's response, the master called him a wicked and lazy servant, and he took the single talent from him and gave it to the first servant, who now held ten talents. Since the third servant could not be trusted with a small amount, any future opportunity was removed. Only proven and trustworthy individuals receive increased responsibilities, which is true both in the secular world and in the Church. We look for people who we can trust to complete tasks to the best of their ability, without complaints or excuses. Every pastor prayerfully seeks parishioners who can be trusted to serve in a manner that reflects both the importance of the task and the love of Christ. To have such people in a congregation is a blessing that keeps giving.

The disobedient servant not only lost what the master gave him, but his excuses also resulted in punishment. The master labeled him worthless and cast him out into a painful state of darkness. If this servant had sought mercy from the master and asked for a second chance, he might have turned things around and found a happier end result, but he refused to confess his failings. Instead, he placed the blame on the master, calling him a hard and demanding man. This story applies to the people who blame God as an unreasonable task master. Instead of being obedient to the Lord and manifest a penitent heart when they sin, their lack of remorse brings judgment upon themselves. In their disobedience, they chose to travel their own path, instead of trusting in God's wisdom and providence. The servant had an opportunity to share in his master's joy, which would have benefited him as a worker, but he refused. Many people cannot imagine how serving the Lord brings joy into their lives. The truth, however, is that blessings come through the giving of ourselves. This, of course, is not the way of the world.

God has placed everyone in a position of trust, and while we wait for our Master's return, we are to invest our lives for Christ and the Church. As his creation, we can only find contentment and joy through a surrendered life. Before sending out his twelve disciples, Jesus told them, "Anyone who does not take his cross and follow me is not worthy of me. Whoever finds his life will lose it, and whoever loses his life for my sake will find it" (Matthew 10:38, 39). There are only two paths we can travel in life. Either we can invest our lives for God, or we walk the road of disobedience.

REFLECTION

- What does it mean to offer yourself up as a living sacrifice acceptable to the Lord?

  To be a living sacrifice for God simply means that we have given up every room of our house. In other words, all that we are and possess is placed in the Lord's hands. In our surrender, we continuously strive to live in the teachings and will of our Creator.

- Identify some ways you have made investments for God.

  As we give thought to the investments that we have made for God, we should also think about the benefits that we derived through these investments. As discovering in the parable, those who were obedient to their master received rewards.

- How can you increase your spiritual investments?

  It is through prayer that God provides opportunities to serve him. The Lord will take the desires of our heart and provide ways that we can work in his vineyard. Our prayers will give us the sensitivity needed to recognize the opportunities that are set before us and the direction that we should follow.

- Do you ever feel that God is too demanding? If so, provide some examples.

  There are times when everyone feels the weight that accompanies serving the Lord. Whether clergy or lay person, the ministry of compassion can often become overwhelming upon our energy and emotions. This is why Jesus often took time away from people for personal rest and renewal. Christians must remember that, although they walk in the Spirit, they are still flesh and blood.

Fourteen

THE GROWING SEED

Text: Mark 4:26–29 (NIV)

> He also said, "This is what the kingdom of God is like. A man scatters seed on the ground. Night and day, whether he sleeps or gets up, the seed sprouts and grows, though he does not know how. All by itself the soil produces grain—first the stalk, then the head, then the full kernel in the head. As soon as the grain is ripe, he puts the sickle to it, because the harvest has come."

This allegory, only recorded by Mark, is rooted in the *Parable of the Sower*. It relates to the growth process of the seed that fell upon good soil and completed at the harvest, implying that the seed is good and fell upon prepared soil. If that were not the situation, the seed could not germinate, and fully develop. The parable reminds us that the growth process is a mystery. Once the seed is scattered, an unexplainable life force takes over.

In certain biblical translations, the word *seed* is sometimes used in a figurative way to denote the prosperity of man (Genesis 3:15; 4:25; 13:15). The Lord's promise to Abraham and his seed, to give them land and make them a great nation, has a dual meaning. It concerns both his natural descendents and those not biologically related, who would share his righteous characteristics (Romans 4:16). Seed is also symbolic of God's Word (Luke 8:5, 11; I Peter 1:23), and preaching is sometimes referred to as sowing seed (Matthew 13:32; I Corinthians 9:11). Jesus compares his death to the sowing of a seed, resulting in new life for his followers (John 12:24). Paul also makes a connection between death and the sowing of seed (I Corinthians 15:36–38).

These symbolic applications of seed in biblical teachings speak to the subject of spiritual regeneration and growth. The Lord planted the seeds of the gospel, which have taken root through Christ's atonement and the movement of the Holy Spirit upon the human heart. As in nature, this process is a mystery, but no one can deny the results. Both in our personal lives and the collective life of the Church, the grain continues to ripen in preparation for God's harvest. In a personal way, we know the spiritual growth that has occurred in our lives. This can be compared to the growth that has taken place throughout the world, as the seed of the gospel has taken root and brought forth new life.

Jesus is the divine seed sent down from heaven, the incarnate Word of God, whose sacrificial death offers life to all people. The death and resurrection of Christ lays the foundation for the work of the Church and God's earthly kingdom in preparation for the Second Advent. As Jesus tarries, God commissioned us to spread the living seed of the gospel. It is through our surrender, confession of faith and acts of love, that we produce grain—first the stalk, then the head, and then the full kernel in the head. Through changed hearts, we become sensitive to others' needs, putting off self that others might know Jesus Christ.

As sowers of God's seed, we must never lose sight of our mission. By following Jesus' example, our primary ministry is the gospel message. Social and healing ministries are unquestionably the will of God, but we must never abandon the good news of Jesus Christ for other forms of outreach. I have always been amazed how buildings and secular matters concern church leaders more than teaching and preaching the gospel. Many churches lose their focus and purpose for existence. As a result, they experience a spiritual decline and membership loss. Some churches become Christian banks, having lost their faith and sense of giving to the needy.

In Revelation, the angel of the Lord told the apostle John to write to seven churches. These communications, found in Chapter Two, expose churches that God called to repentance and change. To the church in Ephesus, John wrote, "You have forsaken your first love. Remember the height from which you have fallen! Repent and do the things you did at first. If you do not repent, I will remove your lampstand from its place" (Revelation 2:4, 5). To the church in Sardis, he wrote these words, "Wake up! Strengthen what remains and is about to die, for I have not found your deeds complete in the sight of my God" (3:2). The church in Laodicea was told, "I know your deeds, that you are neither cold nor hot. I wish you were either one or the other! So, because you are lukewarm, neither hot nor cold, I am about to spit you out of my mouth" (3:15, 16).

As the living body of Jesus Christ, we have the great responsibility of spreading the seeds of the gospel. God commissioned us to preach his message of repentance and reconciliation, emphasizing that our salvation is through God's grace and our personal faith in Jesus Christ. Jesus certainly cares about the whole person, as seen in his discourses and miracles, but his primary mission was spreading the gospel and offering up his life for all sinners. Although we must never cease our social work and other forms of outreach to those in need, the salvation of souls is the primary reason we are called. Let us not forget that our compassion for others has its source in the gospel message. We love and reach out to others because of the love of Christ in us. Reaching out to those in need is a natural response for our Savior's disciples. We care because God has given us the heart of his Son.

This lesson is not about buildings, church denominations, or traditions. The kingdom of God is not an earthly structure or secular organization. Instead, it is the movement of the Holy Spirit upon the hearts of people, bringing life, growth, and maturity to the seeds planted by God and his Church. As planters of the seed, we have our part, but it is the Lord who completes the process. We do not have the power to grant people salvation. As disciples, our message, Christian example and prayers, lead individuals to Jesus Christ. Although God has called us to plow, plant, and water, he performs the miracle of spiritual regeneration. Like the work of nature, salvation is a mysterious and unseen process that is beyond our ability and control. Jesus teaches us that salvation is a matter of the heart because it is the heart that either receives or rejects the seed. In nature, a life force within the seed is the catalyst that brings germination. Likewise, the spiritual life force in the gospel quickens the human heart. In both situations, the process is dependent upon certain conditions, as well as God's grace and power.

In this parable, Jesus reveals the importance of sowing seed, but this raises a crucial question for the Church. Are we planting true gospel seeds, or is the message of Jesus Christ becoming obscured by humanism, secular thought, and false doctrine? These are only a few problems found within the Church. Other problems include legalism, the intentional distortion of Scripture for personal advantage, and the extreme liberalism that we find in some church circles. Jesus charged the Jewish leaders with a form of legalism and work-righteousness that falsely interpreted the Hebrew Scriptures for self-glorification and personal gain. They composed rules that the common people could neither understand nor follow. In this system, one earned their way into the kingdom through obedience to man's laws. The leaders, of course, were the pious experts whose legal authority and adherence pleased God. These false seeds prevented people from experiencing the Lord's mercy, as well as the understanding necessary for spiritual development. Unfortunately, legalism continues today in many of our churches. I encountered this blight on every level of church ministry, and it is difficult to confront and eradicate, primarily because it feeds upon human pride and self-will.

Often used in a political context, liberalism is another word familiar to us. In the Church, it sometimes refers to the belief that God accepts any lifestyle. In other words, how can the Lord condemn human desires and actions that some people fail to see as sinful? The assumption is that a God of forgiveness and love will not eternally punish those he created. This belief takes many forms, with debates found within and between religious groups. Although there are many issues relating to liberalism, those of a sexual nature lead heated discussions and ignite internal conflicts.

Whether it is humanism, legalism, false doctrine, liberalism, or the influences of unchanged hearts, the Church is plagued with individuals and groups who spread seeds of destruction and discontent. While parish pastors can bring change through education, it is an arduous process that meets strong resistance. Many churches dismiss pastors who try to redirect the erroneous paths of their congregation. In some cases, the pastors instigate the problem through their ignorance or lack of patience. For whatever reason, scriptural misinterpretations lead to devastating results, with inadequate education and narrow thinking often being the culprit. Nothing can replace a solid theological education for pastors and church leaders. This is why many churches are developing education programs for lay leaders that provide doctrinal beliefs and a foundational understanding of scripture. Sowing good seed must be our focus, which means properly interpreting and communicating God's Word.

This parable ends with the harvest. At a particular time, God will conclude that the field is ready for harvest, and this will usher in the eternal kingdom. No one knows when this will occur, for the decision lies only with the Father. The harvest metaphor, a graphic and repetitious theme in the New Testament, is aimed at keeping us vigilant in our spiritual journey.

REFLECTION

• Do you ever get discouraged with your spiritual growth? If so, provide some examples.

> It is not unusual for people to report discouragement with their spiritual development. While this may reveal a particular problem, it is normal for us to experience these feelings. Sometimes we need to encourage ourselves by looking back and seeing just how far we have traveled since receiving Christ into

our lives. There will always be a tension between where we are in our spiritual journey and where we desire to be. This is probably a good place, for it keeps us moving onward and upward.

• What are some ways that you can nurture the seed God planted in your heart?

The nature of seed is to bring forth life, and then to grow and develop. When we are spiritually born, our sights are also on growth and maturity. This is accomplished through many sources and opportunities, all of which are mentioned in the teachings of this book. What is important, is that we never lose the desire to grow in the image of our Savior. If complacency comes into our life, the growth within us will certainly be in peril.

• How should we understand the growth process of new Christians? Explain our ministry to these individuals.

New Christians can be compared to recently born infants, who need years of parental assistance to develop and maintain their health. As children grow, they often falter and experience setbacks. This is also true of babes in Christ, which is why we must be understanding and patient as they struggle to mature. This lesson should also be applied to our lives.

• Why is patience important in our relationships?

When considering patience in our relationships, we need to reflect upon God's patience toward us and the grace that it has made possible. Without divine patience, we would not know the love and forgiveness of our Savior. This truth provides an important insight for the benefit of all relationships.

Fifteen

THE TWO DEBTORS

Text: Luke 7:41–43 (NIV)

"Two men owed money to a certain money-lender. One owed him five hundred denarii, and the other fifty. Neither of them had the money to pay him back, so he canceled the debts of both. Now which of them will love him more?" Simon replied, "I suppose the one who had the bigger debt cancelled." "You have judged correctly," Jesus said.

This lesson was taught in response to the unforgiving heart of a Pharisee named Simon. To understand this parable within its context, we must begin our reading at verse thirty-six of Chapter Seven and continue through verse fifty. These verses describe events that occurred when Jesus accepted Simon's invitation to dine at this house. While Jesus reclined at Simon's table, a woman, hearing that Jesus was going to be there, visited him and brought an alabaster jar of perfume to anoint his feet. It is recorded that this woman, a known prostitute, bent over Jesus. As her tears wet his feet, she wiped them away with her hair. Then, she kissed his feet and cleansed them with the perfume.

When Simon observed the woman touching Jesus, he was appalled and felt disgust toward both the woman and Christ. Simon thought that if Jesus were a true prophet, he would know the woman's reputation and refuse any interaction with her. Jesus knew what pervaded Simon's thoughts, and he addressed the issue with a succinct, and yet, powerful lesson that ended with a question directed at his host. What Simon learned that day shook the foundations of his spiritual world.

The Pharisees looked upon certain sins as excluded from God's grace. They also believed that being in the presence of certain people defiled them spiritually. They considered women who engaged in sexual sins, like prostitution, the worst of sinners. Simon could not comprehend anyone allowing a prostitute to touch them, particularly a prophet or religious teacher. However, Simon did not know that he invited the Son of God to his home, who has the power to forgive sins and would soon sacrifice his life for all sinners. Without realizing the true identity of Jesus, Simon found himself confronted with a lesson that challenged his spiritual intellect and his concept of divine grace.

Simon believed that his righteousness was found in physically separating himself from those perceived to be sinners and violators of God's laws. He refused to consider that God's law is love for all people, and that people can change through repentance and the power of faith. This radical teaching was difficult for him to grasp. But, isn't this still the situation today? My prison chaplaincy was a growth process for me, for not only did I learn about inmate dynamics, but I also gained insight into societal attitudes toward the incarcerated. Many people believe that prisoners are hopeless incorrigibles who do not deserve God's grace. Some individuals think that convicted criminals should never serve the church or even profess their faith in community churches. I encountered these sentiments when I accompanied the prison sanctuary choir into community churches. At one particular church, I was shocked to learn that some of the church leadership refused to attend the choir program, believing that convicted criminals had no right to share any type of ministry. This response made me question the spiritual state of the entire congregation. It is amazing how people can attend worship services for years, yet miss the message of the gospel.

People forget that Jesus came seeking the lost and that the Church is a hospital for the sick. When religious leaders complained that Jesus spent too much time with sinners, he immediately replied, "It is not the healthy who need a doctor, but the sick. But go and learn what this means: I desire mercy, not sacrifice. For I have not come to call the righteous, but sinners" (Matthew 9:12, 13; Luke 5:31). This statement forced the Jewish leaders to look at themselves, knowing that they were sinners as well.

Ever since Luke wrote this text, the woman in this parable has had an impact upon the lives of readers. She came to Jesus in humility and with a repentant heart. She fell at Christ's feet with tears flowing from her eyes, wiping his feet with her hair, the crown of her beauty. Many scholars believe that her alabaster jar of perfume was worth a week's wages. What more could she have done to honor Jesus, seek forgiveness, and a new lease on life? This, however, failed to move Simon, who refused to believe that she could be forgiven and become a changed person. Her sins, as well as his own, blinded him to God's forgiving love. This ancient lesson translates well into contemporary times because many people, including Christians, find difficulty moving beyond a person's past life, and in some cases, the mistakes of the past become a life sentence. Rather than reaching out in love and forgiveness, the Church often slays its wounded. Instead of praising the Lord for another's spiritual birth, resentment breeds because such a person receives forgiveness and equal love from God.

Jesus responded to Simon's criticism by saying, "You did not give me water for my feet, but she wet my feet with her tears and wiped them with her hair. You did not give me a kiss, but this woman, from the time I entered, has not stopped kissing my feet. You did not put oil on my head, but she put perfume on my feet. Therefore, I tell you, her many sins have been forgiven— for she loved much. But he who has been forgiven little loves little" (Luke 7:44–48). When individuals acknowledge the extent of their sins and the need for God's forgiving grace, they tend to be less judgmental of others. This is particularly true if they committed gross sins. Also, it is not unusual for people to become very emotional when experiencing God's forgiveness. In fact, the woman's tears in this parable are an example of both the remorse and joy that results from inner cleansing and spiritual regeneration. In some church congregations, it is quite common to see members express outward emotion when someone testifies about their forgiveness and God's saving grace. My first pastorate was such a church and, although it was a new experience for me, I found it to be sincere and spiritually refreshing. In some churches, any manifestation of emotion is frowned upon and viewed as a character weakness.

To condemn others is to dismiss the love and power of God in their lives. If we know that Christ died for all people and God seeks to save the worst of sinners, how can we desire their destruction? We must remember that no one is beyond salvation, and God is the only judge of the human heart. Our commission is to communicate God's love and forgiveness to the world, a calling which Simon refused to accept. Like many people today, his pride and self-will became an obstacle.

Simon probably invited Jesus to his home with ulterior motives. He was certainly curious about Jesus, who spoke with authority and seemed to have answers concerning life and death. Also, Jesus' large following concerned the religious elite. Possibly encouraged by other religious leaders, Simon may have agreed to obtain information about Jesus to use against him at a later date. But regardless of his motives, Simon found himself confronted with a lesson that contradicted his beliefs and understanding of grace. This undoubtedly placed him in a position of confusion and self-examination. Simon discovered that forgiveness is not negotiable, and God forgives everyone who comes to him in humility and with a penitent heart. Also, he learned that holding a religious office means nothing if the heart has not been changed. Jesus let Simon know that our mission is one of mercy, not self-righteousness and separation from others. Like Jesus, we are to meet people wherever they are in life, so that they might know God's love and power. We must not separate ourselves from others, including the worst of sinners. It is not known how Simon responded to the Lord's lesson, but Jesus gave him the opportunity to change his life. Through divine inspiration, this same lesson challenges us today.

REFLECTION

• How do we know that we have forgiven another person? Is it possible to forgive someone from the heart? Is forgiving others immediate or a process? Does forgiveness necessarily mean forgetting?

> Jesus said that we know we have passed from death to life when we are able to love and forgive all people. Apart from God's love and mercy, forgiveness is not possible. We should always petition the Lord for a forgiving heart, knowing that our own forgiveness is dependent upon us forgiving others. The scriptural teachings relating to this truth are often ignored by individuals and the Church. Although it is personal desire and persistent prayer that remove the barriers which prevent forgiveness, we should remember that this is a process. We may not completely forget another person's offense, but we can forgive them from the heart.

• What do the Scriptures say about judging others? Is there ever a time when we must judge another person? What is the difference between judging the person, as opposed to their actions?

> Our Savior teaches that we are not to judge others, or we ourselves will be judged by God. There are times, however, when we must make judgments concerning the actions and lifestyles of individuals in order to prevent us from falling into sin. There is a difference between tearing a person down before other people and condoning or submitting to their sinful influences.

Sixteen

THE GOOD SAMARITAN

Text: Luke 10:25–37 (NIV)

On one occasion an expert in the law stood up to test Jesus. "Teacher," he asked, "what must I do to inherit eternal life?" "What is written in the Law?" he replied. "How do you read it?" He answered: "'Love the Lord your God with all your heart and with all your soul and with all your strength and with all your mind'; and, 'Love your neighbor as yourself.'" "You have answered correctly," Jesus replied. "Do this and you will live." But he wanted to justify himself, so he asked Jesus, "And who is my neighbor?" In reply Jesus said: "A man was going down from Jerusalem to Jericho, when he fell into the hands of robbers. They stripped him of his clothes, beat him and went away, leaving him half dead. A priest happened to be going down the same road, and when he saw the man, he passed by on the other side. So too, a Levite, when he came to the place and saw him, passed by on the other side. But a Samaritan, as he traveled, came where the man was; and when he saw him, he took pity on him. He went to him and bandaged his wounds, pouring on oil and wine. Then he put the man on his own donkey, took him to an inn and took care of him. The next day he took out two silver coins and gave them to the innkeeper. 'Look after him,' he said, 'and when I return, I will reimburse you for any extra expense you may have.' "Which of these three do you think was a neighbor to the man who fell into the hands of robbers?" The expert in the law replied, "The one who had mercy on him." Jesus told him, "Go and do likewise."

The Jewish leaders, including the scribes who were the legal minds of their day, always scrutinized and questioned Jesus. Over the years, Judaism attributed various duties to the scribes, such as keeper of important documents and copier of the law. But it was their expertise on Mosaic Law that gave them positions of power. Jesus told this parable in response to a *test question* posed by a scribe. Actually, the scribe asked Jesus two questions: What must I do to inherit eternal life, and who is my neighbor? The first question implies that a system of works is necessary for salvation, whereas, the second question relates to the classification of people. The latter question alludes to some people being placed outside the definition of *neighbor*.

In response to the first question, Jesus told the scribe to state the Law. Without any problem, the man quoted the Law verbatim. He told Jesus that eternal life came to those who faultlessly loved God and their neighbor. Jesus agreed, but the scribe continued to question him. "Who is my neighbor?" asked the man. This inquiry took the conversation to another level because the Jews saw Samaritans and uncircumcised Gentiles as beyond the scope of God's saving grace. They were not God's chosen people and therefore, not true neighbors in terms of love and outreach. With Jesus being a Jew, the scribe anxiously awaited his teaching on the matter. What he was about to learn would shatter his legalistic mind and ethnocentrism.

Declassification is a central theme in Jesus' teachings. God's love is unconditional, universal, and excludes no one. In this illustration, Jesus not only gives *love* a new definition, but he also uses someone considered to be unclean by the Jews to represent God's example of love. The Jews looked upon the Samaritans with disgust because they were not pure Israelites, but rather a mixed race that resulted after Assyria captured Israel's ten northern tribes in 722 B.C.

This parable's setting is the road from Jerusalem to Jericho, a seventeen-mile stretch infested with robbers and other criminals. Due to the many assaults and killings, the local people called this ancient highway the Bloody Road. Jesus chose this location for the four characters in his story.

The lesson is about a Jewish traveler, journeying to Jericho, who was viciously attacked, robbed, stripped of his clothing, and left along the road. The first individual to pass by was a priest who, after seeing the man, crossed to the opposite side of the road and continued on his way. The second man was a Levite. The Levites served as temple guards, teachers, and judges, but like the priest, he detoured around the robbery victim. The only man who assisted the bleeding man was a Samaritan, a person considered an outcast by Jews. This Samaritan immediately stopped and with compassion, administered medical care. In doing so he risked his life, because he could have been targeted by criminals, or even blamed for the robbery had others come upon the scene at that moment. However, this good man only saw human need, and without hesitation, he responded.

We learn that the Samaritan poured oil and wine on the man's wounds and placed him on his own donkey, while he walked. He took the victim to an inn, where he once again tended to the man's wounds. The Samaritan then provided the innkeeper with two silver coins, asking him to care for the injured man. Before leaving the inn, the Samaritan told the innkeeper that he would return and compensate him for additional expenses. At this point, the Samaritan could have retreated from more involvement in the victim's situation, but his compassion continued after he brought the man safely to the inn. Rather than do just enough to satisfy his conscience, his love had no limits. He wanted to be certain that he did all he could for the injured man.

Thinking that he could trap Jesus, the scribe instead learned a piercing lesson. Rather than placing Jesus in a religious entanglement, he was suddenly confronted with his own hypocrisy, which was Jesus' intent. We never hear the scribe's response to Jesus' story, whether he hardened his heart or accepted this teaching. We do know that Jesus planted the seed for spiritual transformation.

The Samaritan's story challenges us to look at our lives. We, who claim to walk with Christ, often set boundaries and conditions on our love and ministry to others, particularly toward those who are different from us. Like the priest and Levite in the tale, we are sometimes guilty of walking away from the diseases of humanity. We claim to follow Jesus, but what does our life truly reflect? Are we conscious of the needs around us? Do we treat strangers as undeserving of our sensitivity and compassion? As the body of Christ, we must first possess the desire to be healers. So, who is our neighbor? Maybe we should reverse the question by asking, who is not our neighbor? Jesus tells us that we are all equally loved by God. With the passion of Christ, we find a universal atonement that reaches the darkest places in life. As such, we only share the nature and mission of Jesus Christ when our love is infinite and unconditional. It is a love void of geographical borders, and one that seeks peace rather than conflict, in which the strong protect the weak. Jesus repeatedly teaches that whatever we do for the needy, we do it for him. In other words, we share his compassion, burden and mission.

The scribe learned that inheriting eternal life is not a matter of adhering to formulated religious laws. Instead, it rests in a heart that lives outside of self, one transformed by the love and power of God. Eternal life is found in sharing the mercy of God in a world suffering from the sins of inhumanity. Jesus told the scribe to live the Samaritan's example, showing love to all people, including one's perceived enemies. Our Savior gives us this same message.

REFLECTION

• What is the extent of your outreach to others? Do you set boundaries and limits? Have you ever made an effort to touch the lives of people outside your spiritual, cultural, and racial circles? If so, what were the circumstances and results?

> We have a tendency to gravitate toward those with whom we feel comfortable, without considering the benefits that are possible through a wider fellowship. We have all experienced gatherings where people clump together in small groups, rather than making an effort to become acquainted with other people. Whether intentional or not, Christians set limits on their outreach by the social boundaries they set. The Lord wants us to move beyond our comfort zones for the purpose of shared blessings. It is through diversity that God opens our life to the fullness of his grace.

• Do you pray about your struggles with apathy and prejudice? How can we develop the unconditional and universal love that Jesus requires of us?

> Although it may be painful for us to admit, we occasionally struggle with apathy and some degree of prejudice. God leads us down the path of discernment, that we might love individuals from every walk of life. Regardless of our birthplace or culture, everyone is God's child and therefore equally loved. We must make every effort to confront both apathy and prejudice through prayer and concrete initiatives.

Seventeen

THE FRIEND AT MIDNIGHT

Text: Luke 11:5–8 (NIV)

> Then he said to them, "Suppose one of you has a friend, and he goes to him at midnight and says, 'Friend, lend me three loaves of bread, because a friend of mine on a journey has come to me, and I have nothing to set before him.' Then the one inside answers, 'Don't bother me. The door is already locked, and my children are with me in bed. I can't get up and give you anything.' I tell you, though he will not get up and give him the bread because he is his friend, yet because of the man's boldness he will get up and give him as much as he needs."

Jesus shared this parable to answer the disciples' concerns and questions about prayer. They knew that John the Baptist taught his followers how to pray, and they wanted Jesus to do the same for them. It is uncertain how spiritual these men were prior to meeting Jesus, but they most likely knew prayers common to Judaism. The disciples often observed Jesus pray and were moved by the way he approached God. Jesus' prayers emanated from this heart and were filled with emotion and burden for the people. His prayers were not memorized or read from a text. Watching Jesus, the disciples observed a communication with God that they wished to emulate, and they asked him for guidance.

I identify with our Lord's apostles in their quest for a meaningful prayer life. Although my childhood was rooted in the Church, I was in my thirties before my prayers reflected my true feelings and needs. In previous years, my prayers were mechanical in nature, with little depth given to my struggles and relationships. With Jesus, the apostles witnessed prayer that was both personal and conversational, and they desired this same intimate relationship with God. If only Christians would be moved toward this end. During my twenty-three years of ministry, few people made inquiries relating to prayer. I would like to think that the effectiveness of my ministries was the reason for this, but somehow I doubt this was the case.

Jesus answered their concern by sharing essential elements of prayer. Today, we refer to these acknowledgments and petitions as the Lord's Prayer. Although most people grew up with this prayer, not everyone ponders the true meaning of the words. The Lord's Prayer contains the following parts:

- Acknowledgment of God as Father
- Confession of God's holiness
- Petition for God's earthly kingdom and will
- Request for daily provisions
- Seeking forgiveness for sins
- The need and promise to forgive others
- Asking God for strength to resist temptation
- Petition for the deliverance from personal evil
- Praise for God's eternal power and glory

After this discourse, Jesus told his disciples the parable of the *Friend at Midnight*. This short story reveals a fundamental truth, being the need for persistence in our prayer life. Unlike the homeowner in our lesson, God is never annoyed with our persistence. Jesus simply used a human analogy to convey his point. In other words, if sinners respond to persistence for the wrong reasons, how much more will God respond to those who call upon him with their concerns and requests for spiritual gifts?

Persistent prayer bares the heart's burden, and this speaks to God's compassion. However, Jesus makes it clear that we must pray for gifts that transform us and allow us to minister to others. We are assured that God answers our prayers when we seek the presence and power of the Holy Spirit, who enables us to grow into the image of Jesus, which is the image of a loving and forgiving heart clothed in humility. Jesus uses the words *ask, seek,* and *knock* to emphasize the need for persistence in praying for the Holy Spirit's gifts (Matthew 7:7, 8).

To be persistent is to have a driving desire that is resolute. When examining our personal lives, we become aware of the times we stood firm and resisted giving in to failure. Whether it was a family crisis, an academic challenge, an employment situation, or a financial difficulty, we were tenacious in our quest to succeed. If it were not for my persistence, I would never have accomplished my personal and career goals. In all my endeavors, I prayerfully stayed the course, while seeking God's will. I also prayed that if my pursuits were wrong, then the Lord would give me a new direction. In fact, when writing this book, my prayers were in this context. This is not to say that my life's journey has been without discouragement and trials. On the contrary, I encountered obstacles at each turn in the road. Years ago, someone asked me to name the most encouraging and influential person in my life. I thought of my mother, who died when I was in my thirties. She was a woman of deep faith who persistently prayed for me. But it was the Lord who carried me each step of the way, providing the strength and fortitude to accomplish the tasks set before me.

One cannot meet accomplishments without persistence, and this applies to our spiritual life, in which prayer is both essential and crucial. God has a plan for every person and seeks to accomplish his will through us. Wherever we are in life, the Lord calls us as his priesthood. As his disciples, we are spread far and wide, enlisted to be servants along life's pilgrimage. This requires a perseverance that only comes with continuous prayer. Our weaknesses and infirmities may fail us, but with God all things are possible when we persistently pray in accordance with his will. The apostle John wrote, "This is the assurance we have in approaching God, that if we ask for anything according to his will, he hears us. And if we know that he hears us, then we know that we have that we have asked for" (I John 5:14, 15). This passage of scripture has been engraved into my mind. My problem, however, has always been one of patience. It is not always easy to wait upon the Lord, especially if our wait is long and silent.

We must be fervent in our communion with God by making our prayers unrestrained and passionate. Jeremiah said that those who seek the Lord with all their heart will find him (Jeremiah 29:13). King David prayed from the depth of his being. His prayers reveal intense feelings and persistence that radiated from his faith. Our relationship with God and our prayer life are interconnected. Although the ancients did not possess the multitude of books and commentaries we have today, they did have the power of prayer. Like David, the depth of their relationship with the Lord depended upon their steadfast communion with the Lord.

REFLECTION

- How would you explain your prayer life? Are you persistently praying for God's will and the gifts of the Holy Spirit?

  Knowing the importance of prayer in every area of life should move us to examine our approach to God. Do we always pray for the Lord's leading, and are we willing to accept his responses? When it comes to answered prayer, we need to remember that God's wisdom and timing are perfect. Also, what appears to be an unanswered prayer may be a merciful *no* to our request.

• What does our persistent prayer tell God? Why does the Lord promise to give us the gifts of the Spirit?

Even if our requests do not fall within God's will, our persistence speaks of our concerns and the desires of the heart. The Lord will respond to this insistence, either by satisfying our petitions or taking us in another direction. We can be certain that seeking the gifts of the Spirit are within the Creator's will.

Eighteen

THE RICH FOOL

Text: Luke 12:16–21 (NIV)

> And he told them this parable: "The ground of a certain rich man produced a good crop. He thought to himself, 'What shall I do? I have no place to store my crops.' Then he said, 'This is what I'll do. I will tear down my barns and build bigger ones, and there I will store all my grain and my goods. And I'll say to myself, "You have plenty of good things laid up for many years. Take life easy; eat, drink and be merry.'" But God said to him, 'You fool! This very night your life will be demanded from you. Then who will get what you have prepared for yourself?' This is how it will be with anyone who stores up things for himself but is not rich toward God."

This parable resulted from a person's question about a family financial matter. A man wanted Jesus to address an inheritance issue involving his brother, specifically that the brother should divide the family inheritance with him. It seems that the man's brother refused to cooperate, and Jesus was called to intervene. Although Jesus declined to get involved in the situation, he saw it as an opportunity to teach a lesson on covetousness and the danger in seeking happiness and security in wealth and possessions. However, this parable is neither about the rich versus the poor, nor does it communicate that it is a sin to possess wealth. Rather, it is a story that forces us to examine our thinking and priorities concerning the temporary things in life. Hopefully, the man who sought the Lord's assistance realized that security and happiness are not found in this world.

Preparing for the future is certainly understandable and an important aspect of stewardship. The sin comes when believing that possessions result from our own effort instead of them being gifts from God, which should be shared with others. In addition, there is a false assumption that security accompanies abundance. In other words, the more we have, the better our lives will be. We live in a society that understands the future in terms of investments and portfolios. Rather than looking to the Lord for direction and contentment, we seek out temporary and insecure things in life for answers. We focus upon ourselves and this present age, with little thought given to the needs of others and our eternal future. As Christians, we must lean upon the promises found in the Scriptures, specifically the teachings of Jesus and his apostles. We develop a new understanding of security and happiness only when in faith, we internalize the teachings of Christ. A lack of faith and the need for self-control stand as obstacles in our lives. Few people will admit to being free of financial concerns and the need for personal control over their lives. The problem occurs when we are lured into believing that money and personal control determine our state of security and happiness. When our focus is upon these things, there is little need for God, and here lies the danger.

The lesson's theme is found in verse fifteen. Jesus told the crowd, "Watch out! Be on guard against all kinds of greed; a man's life does not consist in the abundance of his possessions." This is not a proclamation against wealth, for some of God's greatest servants are blessed with worldly riches. However, it is a statement about being rich toward God. One finds real wealth in the richness of the soul, not in earthly possessions. We came into this world naked, and naked, we shall leave it. Therefore, our lives must center upon that which has eternal value, for everything else will pass away. Wealth may give us a present sense of security, but death suddenly strips it away. Mother Theresa was quoted as saying that at the time of death we are all equal. This is a truth that benefits both the wealthy and the poor.

Blessed with good soil and a rich crop, the rich man thought that building larger storage areas would secure his future. He planned out his long retirement with every future need met, and he expected to be happy and carefree. Little did he know how brief his life would be! Many people prepare for the future by simply making worldly investments because they only see themselves in this present life. Do they think that death and accountability is only for others, or do they truly discount an afterlife? Even though Jesus repeatedly warns us about accountability and responsibility, his words often fall upon defensive attitudes.

The Gospels describe a rich young man who came to Jesus wanting to know what he must do to have an eternal life. When Jesus told him that he must obey the commandments, he assured Jesus of his obedience. Then, Jesus told him to sell his possessions and give them to the poor, and he would be given the treasure of heaven. When the young man heard this, he walked away. Knowing that this man owned much wealth, Jesus put his sincerity and faith to the test. After the man departed, Jesus said to his disciples, "I tell you the truth, it is hard for a rich man to enter the kingdom of heaven. Again I tell you, it is easier for a camel to go through the eye of a needle than for a rich man to enter the kingdom of God" (Matthew 19:16–24; Mark 10:24; Luke 18:25).

Not only is covetousness found within rich and powerful circles, but it also tarnishes other segments of society. The world is full of people who have the drive and desire to possess all that they can. The crime rate throughout the world is evidence of this. Our prison populations, which continuously increase, house numerous individuals whose lifestyles encourage violent activity to satisfy their hunger for money and possessions. The covetous heart permeates humanity, not just a particular social group. Our Lord's response to the rich man and his statement to the apostles was a lesson on the dependence and power of wealth over a person's life. The wealthy have a strong tendency to depend upon their riches for security, rather than looking to the love and power of the Creator.

In the parable, the rich man's life centered upon himself, which was an eternal mistake. He believed that everything belonged to him, giving no thought to stewardship, other people, or the uncertainty and brevity of life. In his mind, he was the sole owner of the grain and goods, and he never gave thanks to God, who is the giver of all gifts. His only concern was the desire for more storage areas, without any thought given to the poor, oppressed, and disabled, who live without hope. Blessed with abundance, he saw himself as the only recipient. After all, it was his hard work that placed him in such a good position. To Timothy, Paul wrote, "Command the people to do good, to be rich in good deeds, and to be generous and willing to share. In this way, they will build up treasures for themselves as a firm foundation for the coming age, so that they may take hold of the life that is truly life" (I Timothy 6:18, 19). In the books of Ecclesiastes and Proverbs, King Solomon repeatedly warned the people about the folly of seeking security in possessions. He told them that it demonstrates vanity, and it resembles one chasing after the wind for what cannot be captured.

Few people recognize God as the giver of all good gifts; therefore, they lack thankful hearts. I once taught an adult Sunday school class during the Thanksgiving holiday. At the beginning of the session, I asked the class to make a list of some gifts the Lord graciously gave them. I could see that most were struggling as they wrestled with the question. After a short period of time, I asked for a volunteer to share their list with the class, but no one responded. I realized that they found it difficult to see God as the giver of their gifts. Somehow, they never even considered family and friends as divine blessings. This reality enables us to better understand the character in this parable, being a man who could not see beyond himself. Whether it be relationships, personal health, or material possessions, no gift is possible apart from the Lord. This includes those opportunities that improve our living condition. The greatest gift, of course, is God's saving grace through Jesus Christ.

Before God announced the rich man's death, he called him a fool. The Lord asked, "Who will get what you have prepared for yourself?" Like the Egyptian pharaohs who filled their tombs with possessions to accompany them into the afterlife, many people struggle to let go of their belongings, forgetting that one day it will not be their choice. Giving to others should be the heart's response of living in the love of Christ. Sometimes we forget that what we fail to give during our lifetime will eventually be scrutinized by the one who gave us life and commands that we share it with others.

Continuing the parable's theme, Jesus told his disciples not to worry about their lives. He used nature as a metaphor to demonstrate how God cares for his creation, emphasizing that their lives were more important to God than the created order. He encouraged them to share their valuables with the less fortunate, saying, "Provide purses for yourselves that will not wear out, a treasure in heaven that will not be exhausted, where no thief comes near and no moth destroys. For where your treasure is, there your heart will be also" (32–34).

REFLECTION

- Does God have the right to address our financial issues? Do you seek God's guidance concerning your giving?

  As the one who created us and provides for all of our needs, the Lord has every right to intercede when it comes to our finances. We are merely stewards of all that God has placed in our possession. Seeking his guidance in these matters is important to our well-being and his personal plan for our lives. Our finances are connected to our decision making and the direction we take.

- What are the spiritual dividends that result from reaching out to others? Do you share with your family and friends the blessings that come through giving?

  We will always reap blessings through our giving to others. This is not only a natural law, but it certainly addresses our spirituality. We are to give thought to our giving, particularly how it impacts upon us and touches the lives of others.

Nineteen

THE BARREN FIG TREE

Text: Luke 13:6–9 (NIV)

> Then he told this parable: "A man had a fig tree, planted in his vineyard, and he went to look for fruit on it, but did not find any. So he said to the man who took care of the vineyard, 'For three years now I've been coming to look for fruit on this fig tree and haven't found any. Cut it down! Why should it use up the soil?' 'Sir,' the man replied, 'leave it alone for one more year, and I'll dig around it and fertilize it. If it bears fruit next year, fine! If not, then cut it down.'"

Prior to Jesus telling this parable, some individuals came to him wanting to know if people's tragedies were God's punishment for their sins. Jesus informed his listeners that those who experience misfortunes bear no more guilt than individuals whose lives are less traumatic. He made this reference in response to the Galileans slaughtered by Pontius Pilate as they worshiped and offered up sacrifices in Jerusalem. It is reported that the blood of the Galileans was mixed with the sacrifices. We do not know what led to these executions because no other information is provided.

Thinking that disasters and disease were God's punishment for sin was a common belief among the people. Either you were blessed by God or under some manner of judgment. For example, people believed leprosy to be a scourge resulting from sin and that barren women somehow lost God's favor. These personal connections between tragedy and punishment are carried over from textural interpretations of the Hebrew Bible. Jesus rejected such concepts, making it clear that all people are sinners in need of forgiveness, a message that he continuously emphasized.

This teaching accentuated Israel's barren spiritual state and God's impending judgment if the people refused to repent. But this lesson has personal and international implications today. His rebuke of the people for their spiritual insensitivity is also a present reality. Jesus told the people that even though they could interpret worldly things, their pride and self-will prevented them from understanding the purpose of life. Have things changed today? Our increased knowledge of the world matters little if we fail to recognize God as the creator and sustainer of life.

It is astonishing how far we have come in the pursuit of improving our daily lives. This is particularly true in the fields of science and technology. It seems that there is no limit to what can be accomplished once we develop an objective. For example, computer technology has changed every aspect of life, including business, education, criminal investigation, medicine, and astronomy. Looking at history, one sees that this driven ingenuity has always existed. Jesus acknowledged the understanding people had of the world during his time on earth, but he confronted them on their spiritual insensitivity and failure to comprehend matters of the soul. Although the world has certainly changed since Christ's earthly ministry, the pursuits and priorities of people have not. Our desire to produce spiritual fruit is far less than our secular concerns. While people applaud technology for improving particular aspects of life, it cannot provide the ingredients necessary for spiritual development and the fruit God looks for in our lives.

Jesus used the fig metaphor because it was an analogy that his audience could readily comprehend. Fig trees were a common sight in Palestine, with its fruit being a favorite food source and an important regional commodity. However, the failure of the fig tree was a natural calamity. The people considered their productiveness as a token of peace and a beacon of God's blessing. One could tell if the fig tree would produce fruit by simply looking at the leaves, and once diagnosed, rather than wasting precious soil, unproductive trees were cut down. In the parable, the vineyard owner tried for three years to produce fruit on the tree, even though it seemed to be lifeless. From a spiritual perspective, God also observes our lives for productivity, knowing that our time on earth will soon be complete.

Like the fig tree, God gives us every opportunity to develop and bear the fruit that brings the forgiveness and love of Christ into the world. However, this can only happen when we are spiritually regenerated. In other words, you cannot produce spiritual fruit apart from an inner life. How can we be fruitful for the Lord when we block the movement of the Holy Spirit? In nature, only healthy trees bear fruit, and that same truth applies to our Christianity. We can only receive the nurturing that produces a God-centered life when we are rooted in Christ.

This lesson mentions an intercessor who pleads with the owner for more time. "Sir," the man replied, "leave the tree alone for one more year, and I'll dig around it and fertilize it. If it bears fruit next year, fine! If not, then cut it down." Some biblical scholars believe that the vinedresser is Jesus or the universal Church, which is the body of Christ in the world. Although these hypotheses are plausible, this scriptural verse may also speak to God's patience. Regarding the delay of Christ's return, we recall Peter's words, "The Lord is not slow in keeping his promise, as some understand slowness. He is patient with you, not wanting anyone to perish, but everyone to come to repentance" (II Peter 3:8, 9).

It is divine love that causes Jesus to tarry, but we must not get comfortable thinking that God's patience will continue. The Scriptures emphatically warn that we must prepare for the unexpected return of Christ. When Jesus appears on the clouds of heaven, this grace period will suddenly cease, with the destiny of every person sealed. We must keep vigilant and avoid the influences and temptations that keep us from a committed life. The Church has fallen into a spiritual slumber, and in its effort to please rather than preach the gospel, God's Word has been compromised and diluted. As a reminder, the apostle John wrote these words to the Church in Laodicea: "These are the words of the Amen, the faithful and true witness, the ruler of God's creation. I know your deeds, that you are neither cold nor hot. I wish you were either one or the other! So, because you are neither hot nor cold, I am about to spit you out of my mouth" (Revelation 3:14–16). Jesus told the Laodiceans that he is knocking at their door, seeking to enter the life of the Church.

The Laodicean Church was in Asia Minor, one of the wealthiest commercial centers in the world, which was noted for its banking and clothing manufacturing. This congregation received the severest reprimand of the seven churches mentioned in Revelation. The letter addresses the spiritual tepidness and worldliness that is predicted to prevail in the Church at the end of the age (II Timothy 3:1–8). Becoming self-satisfied and worldly, being a reflection of their wealth and culture, the Laodiceans no longer focused on Jesus and the gospel message as their purpose for being. The text does not detail the church's works, except to say that they were neither cold nor hot. Jesus wished that the people were one or the other. Professing Christians who do not live the life are a damaging witness for Christ and the Church.

The universal Church is full of lukewarm individuals, who fail to produce the fruit associated with the teachings of Jesus and the Christian life.

Some churches are simply social clubs that do not succeed in communicating the gospel, never challenging parishioners to strive toward holiness. These churches lack an outreach to the community because they exist only for themselves, and they will be judged for their refusal to bear fruit.

The prophet Ezekiel addressed the lifeless state of Israel when he said: "The hand of the Lord was upon me, and he brought me out by the Spirit of the Lord and set me in the middle of a valley; it was full of bones. He led me back and forth among them, and I saw a great many bones on the floor of the valley, bones that were very dry. He asked me, 'Son of man, can these bones live?' I said, 'O Sovereign Lord, you alone know' (Ezekiel 37:1–3). Dispersed and no longer bearing fruit, the Israelites lost their spiritual center. Called to be set apart for the Lord, these people were now like dry bones without hope. God told Ezekiel to prophesy their spiritual regeneration (Ezekiel 37:9, 10). Only through renewed faith and surrender to the Lord can we bring life to our dry bones, a hope that God provides for us through his Son.

REFLECTION

- What does it mean to produce fruit for God? Do you believe that individual churches are judged for their spiritual unproductiveness? The Hebrew Bible reports nations being judged by God. Is this possible today?

    Everyone will be judged for the life that they live. Regardless of one's eternal destiny, our sins will be revealed to us. Also, the Church and its leaders will be held accountable for any sin that has caused human suffering. Nations will also come under divine judgment for their promotion of violence and failure to use their God-given resources for the benefit of the world's needy.

- How can individuals and churches be spiritually revived?

    The only way that revival is possible is through repentance, combined with a renewal of faith and a commitment to Jesus Christ and his earthly mission. This change of heart must be sincere and ongoing. In other words, the Lord needs to see signs of a new life and the sanctifying process that seeks after righteousness.

Twenty

THE GREAT BANQUET

Text: Luke 14:16–24 (NIV)

> Jesus replied: "A certain man was preparing a great banquet and invited many guests. At the time of the banquet he sent his servant to tell those who had been invited, 'Come, for everything is now ready.' But they all alike began to make excuses. The first said, 'I have just bought a field, and I must go and see it. Please excuse me.' Another said, 'I have just bought five yoke of oxen, and I'm on my way to try them out. Please excuse me.' Still another said, 'I just got married, so I can't come.' The servant came back and reported this to his master. Then the owner of the house became angry and ordered his servant, 'Go out quickly into the streets and alleys of the town and bring in the poor, the crippled, the blind and the lame.' 'Sir,' the servant said, 'what you ordered has been done, but there is still room.' Then the master told his servant, 'Go out to the roads and country lanes and make them come in, so that my house will be full. I tell you, not one of those men who were invited will get a taste of my banquet.'"

Although there are similarities between this teaching and the parable of *The Wedding Banquet*, distinct differences exist. At the chapter's beginning, Luke reports that a prominent Pharisee invited Jesus as a dinner guest on the Sabbath, and during that visit, Jesus was carefully observed. Reports abounded about Jesus breaking Sabbath laws with his healings and other activities, and the enforcers of the law scrutinized his words and actions.

The Sabbath laws, written and interpreted by Israel's religious elite, prohibited any activity on the Sabbath that could be defined as work. Of course, this required someone to monitor activities and judge what constituted work, and the spiritual leaders appointed themselves to the task. What God intended as a day of rest for people and animals became a complicated practice of laws and violations. A system was crafted that led to a pride-filled hypocrisy that resisted God's invitation for compassion and love toward all people. Israel's leaders possessed all the resources to enable them to understand the essence of God's call, but they had no intention of relinquishing their power and privileges, particularly with the laws they created.

This parable tells the story of countless people who refuse to accept God's call to be a faithful servant in his kingdom. Whether found in the messages of the patriarchs, prophets, apostles, or early disciples, biblical history tells the story of God's invitation being rejected. This is true today as individuals and the Church convey the good news of Jesus Christ. While people conjure up many reasons to refuse God's invitation, they all revolve around pride and self-will. These sins blind us to a meaningful and fulfilled life that the Lord promises.

While the banquet mentioned in this parable may be viewed as ongoing, it symbolically refers to the ushering in of God's eternal kingdom. This event is accompanied by the return of Jesus, the resurrection of those who died in Christ, the rapture of the living saints, and the final judgment. The victory celebration is reserved for those who respond to God's invitation through their repentance and faith in Jesus Christ. As illustrated in this teaching, unparalleled joy awaits those who endure the trials of this life and remain faithful to their Savior. We, along with past saints, eagerly anticipate the celebration of our eternal blessing.

In the parable, the master extended the first invitation to the Jews, those called by God to be a sanctified people. In accordance to his promise to Abraham, God brought forth a great nation from Abraham's seed. Formed to become a holy nation set apart to bring God's grace to humanity, the Israelites were the recipients and keepers of God's commandments and law. Unfortunately, the leaders used the Law to their personal advantage. Their religious rules kept them separated from the common people, and their influences and distortion of God's Word prevented many people from understanding divine forgiveness and reconciliation. Jesus' ministry brought a new message of God's love, which threatened those in power. The leaders refused to accept our Savior's teachings and claims, and they certainly would not give up the system of works righteousness which they supervised and judged.

Many people in today's society create rules for others to follow, and this places them in positions of control, resulting in the judgment of their peers. This problem not only exists in the secular world, but it is also found in the

Church. When the teachings of Christ take a back seat to the declarations of influential members of the congregation, the spirit of love is lost.

The master's second call was to the streets and alleys of the town, to bring in the poor, the crippled, and the lame. Many of these people spent their time in the alleys begging for food and other basic needs to survive. The Pharisees saw these individuals as hopeless sinners and outcasts, and they wanted nothing to do with these people. In fact, some privileged society members believed that touching such outcasts would make them spiritually unclean.

What we see is an apathy toward the poor and needy. Even in some Christian circles, it would be unheard of to reach out and invite such people into Christian fellowship and worship. Yet, the Lord commands his Church to uplift all people, particularly the oppressed. Did the outcasts in our parable respond to the master's invitation? Apparently some of them did, for the servant indicated a partial filling of the banquet hall. Even though they did not know the master, they came to his home out of need. Some people today who have a church affiliation never respond to the Lord's invitation, even though their need is great. On the other hand, there are strangers to the gospel whose sinful lives have been completely offered up to God.

Still seeking to fill his banquet hall, the master's third call went out to the surrounding roads and country lanes, and this invitation seems more aggressive then the others. The words *make them come in* indicate some level of persuasion and urgency. Such is the case with God's invitation to the lost. The recipients of this third call lived the farthest away from the master's house and unfamiliar with the master. While this invitation may have included Jews, it was primarily meant for the Gentiles. Bringing God's Word to all people was Israel's mission, but they failed to see others as God's children.

The will and providence of God may take some twists and turns, but it will never fail. Biblical history reveals that God offers opportunities to individuals, groups and nations, and their refusal to serve is not overlooked. In due time, the Lord replaces those who reject his call, giving their responsibilities to those with obedient hearts. Pastors of congregations recognize the church members who possess a humble spirit, desiring to serve the Lord without recognition and praise. Unfortunately, some individuals either refuse to serve in any capacity or seek praise for everything they do. Others have a church affiliation, but they live outside the grace offered by the Church. Their hearts refuse to enter God's banquet hall, having never experienced the first fruits of the Spirit.

Although we examined God's invitation from three perspectives, God gives one call to humanity. He invites all people to receive his Son as Lord and Savior. The call is now, and through faith, the blessings are realized in the present.

We receive this invitation each day, therefore, we must examine our lives daily by seeking to love God more, totally trusting in his grace and promises. The prelude to God's Great Banquet begins now, for heaven celebrates the salvation of every soul that receives the light of Jesus Christ.

REFLECTION

• How do you understand God's invitation to the Great Banquet? What are the present and future applications of this lesson?

> God's invitation is all-inclusive, with an unconditional love that reaches out to every person and nation. No one is excluded from his mercy, and no sin is outside his willingness and power to forgive. Although his call for righteousness and obedience always existed, it is in the life and death of his Son that we clearly see his love and realize certain hope. The Holy Spirit never ceases to speak to the hearts of sinners, inviting them into an eternal life of perfect peace and joy. This will continue until our Savior's return, offering the message of salvation to the far reaches of humanity. Today truly is the day of salvation, for we do not know what tomorrow will bring.

• Does your life ever reflect excuses and lost opportunities? As the Lord's servant, do you invite people into the Great Banquet?

> Even the most mature Christians find excuses for not responding to God's invitations for spiritual edification and service. These excuses normally relate to attitudes, laziness, and self-centeredness. While no one can or should respond to every request of the Church, we must be careful not to build barriers that leave no room to hear God's voice. It is prayer that will give us the answer as to how we should respond.

Twenty-One

THE LOST SHEEP

Text: Luke 15:3–7; Matthew 18:12–14 (NIV)

> Then Jesus told them this parable: "Suppose one of you has a hundred sheep and loses one of them. Does he not leave the ninety-nine in the open country and go after the lost sheep until he finds it? And when he finds it, he joyfully puts it on his shoulders and goes home. Then he calls his friends and neighbors together and says, 'Rejoice with me; I have found my lost sheep.' I tell you that in the same way there will be more rejoicing in heaven over one sinner who repents than over ninety-nine righteous persons who do not need to repent."

Jesus taught this lesson for the benefit of the Pharisees, who could not understand why he would spiritually defile himself by associating with sinners. The religious leaders even considered Jewish tax collectors sinners because they were pawns of the Roman government and often levied excess fees on people. Although the Pharisees were educated in the Scriptures, these men astonished Jesus because they failed to understand that God called them to seek out the lost and lead them to the Lord.

In a previous section, I briefly mentioned a Pharisaic attitude that I encountered in one of my ministries. When the church board interviewed me for the pastor's position, they informed me of the church's decline in attendance and the need for a community outreach program. After considerable dialogue on this topic, we agreed on various ways to accomplish this task. When I became their pastor, the church implemented an intense visitation program, and our congregation doubled in size within three years. Excitement filled the air as we experienced the movement of the Holy Spirit, but several leaders voiced their concern about the lifestyles of some of the new parishioners, believing that they did not fit into the long-standing fabric of the church congregation. There was even concern that the children of these new folks were a bad influence on the children of our members. It seemed that the new influx of people attending the church shattered the comfort zone established by these leaders. These agitated individuals even accused me of spending more time with the new people than with the pillars of the church.

As difficult as it was, I reminded the leadership that the Holy Spirit led the people to our congregation for pastoral care and spiritual development. I also told them that the Church's mission is to minister to the lost, more explicitly, those living under the power of sin. As countless servants can testify, reaching out to the lost can be a test of our Christian love and patience. Jesus' early followers certainly knew the struggles and trials of evangelism because many were persecuted and even put to death for their ministry to the lost. But we only embody the Church when we move beyond ourselves, meeting people where they are in life. Whether someone is a member of a street gang, a prison inmate, or a professed atheist, the Church is called into the darkest areas of life with the light of the gospel. Jesus left his throne of glory to share his life with all people and to die for the worst of sinners.

It is interesting that we sometimes see people who are outside our family or friendship circles as unworthy of the Church's efforts. However, the opposite feelings occur when we seek the salvation of our parents, siblings, children, or acquaintances. Christ's teachings emphasize that regardless of one's sins, we are all equally loved by God. Just as loving parents desire the best for their children, God offers us a transformed life made possible through his Son. As the Great Shepherd of the flock, Jesus paid the ultimate sacrifice for the sheep, not wishing that any should perish. This is the example and the challenge set before every Christian and the Church.

The message that Jesus conveyed through this parable, albeit brief, contains the essence of the gospel and states our mission as Christians. Jesus uses the biblical symbolism of the shepherd to describe God's relationship with us. Shepherd images invoke thoughts of a provider and caretaker, as well as a protector who defends the sheep against enemies. While Old Testament writers used the shepherd analogy to describe the function of leaders (Jeremiah 23:4), its most important use is in the context of God's relationship with humanity. For example, the prophet Isaiah wrote, "He tends his flock like a shepherd: He gathers the lambs in his arms and carries them close to his heart" (Isaiah 40:11). King David looked to God as his shepherd when he wrote, "The Lord is my shepherd, I shall lack nothing. Even though I walk through the valley of the shadow of death, I will fear no evil, for you are with me" (Psalm 23:1,

4). Jesus referred to himself as the Good Shepherd, stating that he knows his sheep and his sheep know him. He also foretold that he would lay down his life for the sheep (John 10:14).

The shepherd in the parable left the ninety-nine to go after the one lost sheep. This shows that God actively seeks out the lost until they are found. The shepherd does not make distinctions between the sheep because they are all equally important to him. Like a shepherd experiencing anxiety over one lost sheep, God agonizes over every lost soul. The Lord is mindful of his children and immediately knows when we wander off into a dangerous environment. The Holy Spirit relentlessly searches for every lost and dying soul, and when found, God brings them back into the safety of the fold.

If you ever lost something of value, you know the frantic and empty feeling that overcomes you. Having your small child wander away from you in a public place is even more traumatic. Years ago, when my daughter was four years old, this happened to me at a busy shopping mall. I cannot begin to express what I felt while looking for her, until finally a mall employee announced over a loud speaker that they located a lost child. The ten minutes I spent frantically searching for her felt like a lifetime, knowing the dangers that existed. I learned a valuable lesson that day, one that other parents can certainly understand. The world is full of evil forces that seek to rob our families of joy. As we all know, danger exists in some of the most unlikely places. Personal evil often appears as a caring presence, only to wait for an opportune time.

We are God's children, and when we are lost, our heavenly Father experiences these same emotions. God's pain deepens with the thought that we could be lost forever, and this explains the intense joy when we are found. It is a celebration in which all the angels and departed saints take part. Nothing is more important to the Lord than the human life he created. As God's beloved children, we must realize that there is no sacrifice too great when it comes to our salvation. Jesus Christ gave his life for everyone, past, present, and future, and just as the shepherd left the ninety-nine to retrieve one lost sheep, our Savior would have given his life for just one person.

Some pastors wish for large congregations, believing that these ministries are more important, but sometimes God calls us to reach out to just one person who wandered from the Father's care. I often ministered to individuals who lost their way in life. Whether in a community parish or the state prison system, my pastorates were mostly search and rescue missions. These ministries taught me how much God loves every troubled soul, and I now understand that taking up the cross means sharing in God's burden for every lost soul. This type of ministry seldom brings us accolades from our peers, but it does make us one with the Great Shepherd of the flock. There is no greater sense of fulfillment than serving on God's front line, touching the lives of those who have lost their way, and then sharing in their joy when they enter the fold. Every ministry is important, but rescuing the lost has a certain affinity to Christ. This is not to indicate that such missions are without challenges. Like the shepherd in our lesson, it would have been easy to remain in the fold with the other sheep, but he was driven out of love to go look for the one that was lost.

One can interpret the parable's last verse in different ways. Jesus refers to the ninety-nine as the righteous who do not need repentance, but this is problematic if we believe that everyone is a sinner in need of God's forgiving grace. Some suggest that Jesus was alluding to heaven's angels. Others think this a reference to the saved, being those whose sins are covered by Christ's atoning blood. There is also the belief that Jesus was forcing the Pharisees, who considered themselves sinless, to examine their hearts. While all three theories are reasonable, I believe that the ninety-nine, however imperfect, represent those who are saved. Through faith and divine grace, God already declared them righteous, and their continued faith and commitment to Jesus Christ keeps them secure in God's fold. In our churches, these are the individuals who are rooted in faith, resting in the Shepherd's care and protection.

The Pharisees held on to a cold and lifeless religion rooted in self-glorification, legalism, and a loveless apathy for the lost and needy. This is also the story of many professing Christians who separate themselves from the very people God calls them to serve. We read their names on the church rolls and find them in leadership positions, but they never surrendered to Christ's message and mission. They wear the cloak of Christianity, but they do not live the life.

REFLECTION

- What obstacles prevent you from reaching out to the lost, particularly those entrenched in sinful living?

   Although our call is to the lost and dying, it is difficult to walk in life's trenches searching out the wounded. The mere thought of this repels some people. These ministries are not for everyone, but to remove ourselves from the darkest places in life is to reject the commission of Jesus Christ. Our Savior lived and dined with sinners, that he might reveal the glory of God. He knew that ministry is not accomplished from a distance.

- Does your church have a defined and active mission to the lost? Explain the program or your thoughts on why there is no program.

Every church must be a lighthouse and place of refuge in the community. It should also be a base station from which to launch an evangelistic mission to the surrounding area.

• Do the teachings of your congregation emphasize the principles found in this parable?

Every Sunday, church members hear sermons and teachings, but are they related to personal and community needs? Pastors and church leaders are given the responsibility of translating the Scriptures into real-life situations.

• How much personal sacrifice are you willing to endure for the lost?

The Church is not simply a social club for like-minded people. It is the body of Jesus, charged with picking up his cross, even when it brings trials and pain. Let us never take our eyes off of Calvary and the life of the apostles.

Twenty-Two

THE LOST COIN

Text: Luke 15:8–10 (NIV)

> "Suppose a woman has ten silver coins and loses one. Does she not light a lamp, sweep the house and search carefully until she finds it? And when she finds it, she calls her friends and neighbors together and says, 'Rejoice with me; I have found my lost coin.' In the same way, I tell you, there is rejoicing in the presence of angels of God over one sinner who repents."

This parable parallels *The Lost Sheep*, and one can refer back to the *The Lost Sheep* for a broader explanation of the intended lesson. Always concerned with wealth and money, the Pharisees probably found this lesson interesting and gave Jesus their attention, until they grasped its meaning. The lost coin found in this parable is the Greek drachma, the wage paid to a laborer for one day's work. If one considers the ten silver coins to be the woman's savings, then one missing coin would be a significant loss.

Some scholars believe that the woman described in the parable represents Jesus, and the lamp is the illumination of the Holy Spirit, who searches for the lost. Although this interpretation may be different than Jesus' intention, biblical symbols of darkness and light to compare good and evil are well documented. We must remember, however, that most of the people, except for Israel's leaders, to whom Jesus spoke, were uneducated and heard such teachings only once. As such, they probably found it difficult to grasp a parable's main theme, let alone uncover a deep theological meaning. Today, the parables are written down, and we can spend the time necessary to interpret them.

With that said, the urgency of the search and the celebration of finding something lost, is the parable's basic interpretation.

In these few verses, we feel a sense of urgency because the woman immediately began her search when she discovered the coin to be missing. She had little time to waste! She lit a lantern, swept the entire house, and searched carefully until she found it. Having need for a lamp, one might think that this dilemma occurred at night, but this may not be the situation. Many Eastern homes lacked, or had very small windows, making it difficult to see even during daylight hours. Her effort to find the coin is suggestive of God bringing his light into our dark world in his search for the lost.

When the woman found the lost coin, she sighed with relief and invited her friends to share in her joy. The coin was so important that she wanted her friends and neighbors to celebrate with her. To celebrate the recovery of a lost coin may seem extreme, but the woman valued it greatly. In a spiritual sense, many people think that heaven celebrating the salvation of one lost soul is extreme, but this proves how much God loves and values us.

Many people know the feeling of being rescued by God, forgiven of their sins, and being spiritually quickened. This is especially true when someone has spent many years in a lost state. Empowered by the Holy Spirit, there is a sense of release and joy that comes with being set free from the past and given a new lease on life. I occasionally see bumper stickers that read *I Found It!* At first, I failed to understand the meaning of this statement. I later learned that it was a profession of faith in Jesus Christ. Finding the truth in Christ fills us with joy and hope.

When I received Christ into my life at the age of thirty-four, my happiness overwhelmed me, and I wanted to tell everyone about my new birth and life in the Spirit. But I found that the change in my life disconcerted some family members and friends, who were not Christians. A few people thought that I lost something, rather than finding the one who would forever change my life. As a pastor, it is exciting to see the joyful responses of people who find Jesus Christ after hearing the gospel. My exhilaration continues as I watch them develop into the maturity of our Savior's love and burden for others.

Although the woman in the parable knew her coin was recoverable, she still felt relief when she actually held it in her hand. When something is lost, its value does not diminish. Regardless how long a person is lost or where they have been, their value before God never diminishes. Some people struggle to find value in a lost sinner, particularly if the sinner's life reflects a criminal nature, but God sees everyone as redeemable and worthy of forgiveness and a new life. Even though the woman's loss still left her with nine silver coins, she kept her focus upon the one that was lost. Spiritually, no matter how many people enter God's kingdom, the Lord desires to find every lost soul. We sometimes detour around those who offend us, but in Christ we find a suffering Servant who walked in the dredges of this world, touching the untouchables.

REFLECTION

- Explain what you experienced when you found the truth offered by Jesus Christ. Where were you in your life's journey when God found you?

  No one is at the same place in life when they receive Christ into their life. Those who have grown up in a church environment may never have lost faith. Others report that they came to the Lord when their lives became shattered. Whatever one's experience has been, it is a story that should be told to help communicate hope to troubled souls.

- What efforts have you made to search for lost sinners?

  Life is a highway that takes us to many places, and along the roadways we encounter many lost people. Much of our ministry comes naturally by simply allowing Jesus Christ to shine through us. Rather than searching, the Lord often brings individuals into our presence. Through the providence of God, people are led to those who can give them encouragement and hope. This does not mean that we close the door to God's commission and leading.

- How do you communicate the gospel to family and friends who are not Christians?

  Sharing Christ with our families can be very sensitive, primarily because we do not want to alienate those whom we love. Family members are often confused about the changes that have taken place in us. It is normally best to simply be a Christian, rather than wear it on our sleeve. Through our prayers and love, combined with the witness of our inner peace and joy, others see Christ in us. This is not to say that openly talking about our faith should be avoided, but it must be done with loving care.

Twenty-Three

THE LOST SON

Text: Luke 15:11–32

Jesus continued: "There was a man who had two sons. The younger one said to his father, 'Father, give me my share of the estate.' So he divided his property between them. Not long after that, the younger son got together all he had, set off for a distant country and there squandered his wealth in wild living. After he had spent everything, there was a severe famine in that whole country, and he began to be in need. So he went and hired himself out to a citizen of that country, who sent him to his fields to feed pigs. He longed to fill his stomach with the pods that the pigs were eating, but no one gave him anything. When he came to his senses, he said, 'How many of my father's hired men have food to spare, and here I am starving to death! I will set out and go back to my father and say to him: Father, I have sinned against heaven and against you. I am no longer worthy to be called your son; make me like one of your hired men.' So he got up and went to his father. But while he was still a long way off, his father saw him and was filled with compassion for him; he ran to his son, threw his arms around him and kissed him. The son said to him, 'Father, I have sinned against heaven and against you. I am no longer worthy to be called your son.' But the father said to his servants, 'Quick! Bring the best robe and put it on him. Put a ring on his finger and sandals on his feet. Bring the fattened calf and kill it. Let's have a feast and celebrate. For this son of mine was dead and is alive again; he was lost and is found.' So they began to celebrate. Meanwhile, the older son was in the field. When he came near the house, he heard music and dancing. So he called one of the servants and asked him what was going on. 'Your brother has come,' he replied, 'and your father has killed the fattened calf because he has him back safe and sound.' The older brother became angry and refused to go in. So his father went out and pleaded with him. But he answered his father, 'Look! All these years I've been slaving for you and never disobeyed your orders. Yet you never gave me even a young goat so I could celebrate with my friends. But when this son of yours who has squandered your property with prostitutes comes home, you kill the fattened calf for him!' 'My son,' the father said, 'you are always with me, and everything I have is yours. But we had to celebrate and be glad, because this brother of yours was dead and is alive again; he was lost and is found.'"

The parable of *The Lost Son*, often referred to as *The Prodigal Son*, strikes at the heart of the gospel message, which is forgiveness. Although the wandering son caused his father sorrow and pain, the father immediately forgave him upon his return home. The son repented of his sins and returned in humility, and his father restored him into his household. However, another essential message is found with the older brother, who was jealous over the attention his father gave to the younger son.

This lesson begins with an inheritance issue and a request made by the younger son. The Jewish inheritance laws stated that when there were two sons, the eldest received two-thirds of the estate, and the younger received the remaining third. With permission, the sons could receive the shares while the father lived, and this is exactly what occurred. The younger son received his share of his father's estate, upon which he left home. Jesus tells us that he traveled far from home, to a distant country. Spiritually, this speaks volumes because it tells us that sinful living removes us from God's protection and care. For the unrepentant sinner, it is a journey far from the Father's house. Sin takes many paths, some of which lead into a state of hopelessness. Finding one's way back may be an arduous journey that is filled with obstacles.

Why did the father not stop his son from leaving home? Well, the son reached an age that permitted him to make his own decisions. Besides, like most people, he needed to learn the hard way. Even if his father tried to offer his younger son advice, it would fall upon deaf ears and be ignored. He probably left home because he grew tired of parental restraints and wanted independence and to be his own master. Staying home meant following his father's rules, and he refused to do that. Many of life's lessons are learned the hard way. Our pride and need for control always get in the way of reason, and this was the situation with the younger son.

Over a period of time, the son squandered his entire inheritance, everything his father gave him. Jesus also tells us that a famine spread across the land, and there was no place for the younger son to get help. He was without money or food, and this placed him in a perilous situation. Again, we find a spiritual analogy because the world cannot supply our spiritual and eternal needs. Countless people venture into the world seeking fulfillment and happiness, only to realize that the things of this life cannot satisfy the void they feel. The son cried out that he was starving to death, which is the reality of every person who seeks a life without God. It is sad to see people reach such a place, knowing that the suffering was avoidable by trusting in God's wisdom and care.

At this point, the son acknowledged his destitute state, placing the blame upon himself. He made no effort to blame others for his anguish. He admitted his sins and knew that he needed to return home to his father. He desired the forgiveness that would reconcile him with his father, and he knew that his father's surplus would meet all of his needs. This same truth applies to those who acknowledge their sins, seeking the forgiveness that reconciles them with God and returns them to the Father's house. Apart from God's grace and the gift of Jesus Christ, everyone would be lost in their sins. To the church in Rome, Paul wrote, "All have sinned and fall short of the glory of God, and are justified freely by his grace through the redemption that came by Christ Jesus" (Romans 3:23, 24). In his letter to scattered Christians, Peter said, "For you were like sheep going astray, but now you have returned to the Shepherd and Overseer of your soul" (I Peter 2:25). Although our sins may be many, our return to God is simply a matter of the heart. One of life's tragedies is the belief that certain sins cannot be forgiven, and that one's sinful life has brought them to a place of no return.

According to the parable, the son was a distance from the house when the father saw him returning home, and in his joy, the father ran to meet him. It is apparent that the father's vigilance never wavered. This is also true with God. His watchful eyes always search for those who wander from his loving care. Even in our rebellion, the Holy Spirit speaks to our hearts and minds, lighting the path to the Father's house where hope is kept alive. It is not the Lord who leaves us, but rather we who choose to go our own way.

When the son returned, the father ordered a celebration and feast. He gave his younger son several gifts—a robe, sandals, and a ring, which confirmed the father's love and the son's renewed standing in his father's house. In ancient times, these gifts were symbols of a son's position within the household. The father wanted his son to know that he was completely forgiven and restored to his former standing. When we return to God, he does not question or lecture us about our past sins. Instead, the Lord rejoices that it was our heart's desire to return home. Unlike those who seem to revel in reminding us of our past, the Scriptures tell us that God completely covers over our past sins. When my life changed, there were a number of people who would occasionally let me know about my previous lifestyle. Even after thirty-three years, I still hear some murmurs.

Now, we cannot forget the older brother who refused to take part in the celebration. He was jealous, resentful, and angry, because of the attention that his younger brother received. After all, he never left the father, and in his mind he remained obedient and did what was expected of him. Unlike his guilty younger brother, he never wasted his inheritance on wild living and prostitutes. The older sibling thought his brother's sins were unforgivable, and that he deserved the pitfalls that befell him. This saddened the father, and he reassured his older son of his love for him. Yet, the father reminded him that his younger son, who once was dead, was now alive. How could they not be joyful and celebrate? Many parents can identify with the pain of having a child who lost their way. Whether through drugs, alcohol, or some other way, the concern for wayward children is relentless. Then, when positive changes develop, the joy of parents cannot be contained. When we truly love one another, our heart's desire is to celebrate what has taken place.

The older brother's negativity reminds us that although someone is physically at home, he can still be lost. There are individuals today who, although members of the institutional church, are lost in pride, jealousy, and resentment. Sometimes considered *pillars* in their congregation, they know the Lord's teachings on forgiveness but refuse to put them into practice. The older brother not only refused to forgive his sibling, but he also boasted about his faithfulness to his father. As Jesus points out, many sins come from an unforgiving heart.

While writing on this parable, I recalled a positive experience that I had in my last parish. A local prison ministry asked me if I could transport county prisoners to our Sunday morning worship services. The director of this ministry had worked with me previously and knew I would be security minded. The warden and court system gave certain work release prisoners permission to attend community worship services with supervision. Although I had no problem allowing these men to worship in the church, I certainly needed the permission and support of the congregation. While they expressed justifiable concerns, the church members reached out to these men and worshipped by their side. Every Sunday morning I went to the county prison and transported five or six inmates to our services. At first, it was rather awkward because neither the congregation nor the inmates knew what to expect. However, within a month, a bond developed between the men and our folks. Through our congregation, the inmates experienced the love of Christ, and our members learned some valuable lessons on accepting and ministering to prodigal sons. Needless to say, we all experienced the gospel's power in the life of the Church.

Our time with these men brought mutual blessings that will hopefully recycle for years to come. Christian ministry requires that we move beyond institutional structures in order to reach those with the greatest needs.

REFLECTION

- What character(s) in the story speak to your life?

    While each of the three characters in this teaching speak to us in some way, the Lord calls us to share in his love for all prodigals. This is true discipleship and the mission of the Church. However, it is not possible without the heart of Christ and the movement of the Spirit. Jealousy and resentment are sins which negatively impact upon our relationship with God and one another.

- Have you ever left the Father's house and traveled to a distant country? What were the circumstances?

    An honest look at our lives will reveal times when we chose to follow our own path. We may not have left the fellowship of believers or severed our relationship with the Lord, but we suppressed the inner voice of the Holy Spirit.

- If you were the father in this parable, how would you respond to both the son's departure and his return home? Do you ever experience jealousy when an outpouring of attention is given to new Christians, particularly those who lived blatantly sinful lives?

    One's answer to this question may require some analysis, at least concerning the younger son's departure. We often allow emotions to control our responses to the disturbing behavior of our children. Can we really say that understanding and love would prevail in such a situation? Parents certainly know the conflicting feelings that surface when raising children. Anger sometimes finds its way into family situations.

Twenty-Four

THE SHREWD MANAGER

Text: Luke 16:1–15 (NIV)

Jesus told his disciples: "There was a rich man whose manager was accused of wasting his possessions. So he called him in and asked him, 'What is this I hear about you? Give an account of your management, because you cannot be manager any longer.' The manager said to himself, 'What shall I do now? My master is taking away my job. I'm not strong enough to dig, and I'm ashamed to beg—I know what I'll do so that, when I lose my job here, people will welcome me into their houses.' So he called in each one of his master's debtors. He asked the first, 'How much do you owe my master?' 'Eight hundred gallons of olive oil,' he replied. The manager told him, 'Take your bill, sit down quickly, and make it four hundred.' Then he asked the second, 'And how much do you owe?' 'A thousand bushels of wheat,' he replied. He told him, 'Take your bill and make it eight hundred.' The master commended the dishonest manager because he acted shrewdly. For the people of this world are more shrewd in dealing with their own kind than are the people of the light. I tell you, use worldly wealth to gain friends for yourselves, so that when it is gone, you will be welcomed into eternal dwellings. Whoever can be trusted with very little can also be trusted with much, and whoever is dishonest with very little will also be dishonest with much. So if you have not been trustworthy in handling worldly wealth, who will trust you with true riches? And if you have not been trustworthy with someone else's property, who will give you property of your own? No servant can serve two masters. Either he will hate the one and love the other, or he will be devoted to the one and despise the other. You cannot serve both God and Money." The Pharisees who loved money, heard all this and were sneering at Jesus. He said to them, "You are the ones who justify yourselves in the eyes of men, but God knows your hearts. What is highly valued among men is detestable in God's sight."

While the language and contradictions in this parable make it difficult to understand, it contains powerful insights into sinful human nature. It addresses the creativity that many people employ to deceive others for personal gain. This parable was certainly a lesson for Israel's self-serving leaders, but the apostles also needed to hear Jesus' words on the deception and greed that often accompanies positions of authority and power. Soon, the apostles would be placed in leadership roles and subjected to the influences and temptations associated with these positions. Even though they would have the authority and power to claim the gospel and lay the foundations of the Church, their character was to be that of a humble servant. So often, people in authority positions start out with good intentions, only to be consumed by ego, power, and greed. Regardless who the person is in a leadership position, these temptations and forces are always present and must be confronted.

Few people are guiltless when it comes to using some manner of manipulation for personal gain. In every aspect of life, including the Church, self-serving individuals distort the truth and take advantage of others to satisfy their need for power and control. This potential exists within everyone because we are not without sin and therefore vulnerable to temptation. Manipulation and deception are fused into the very fabric of our society.

In the parable, Jesus describes how creative people can be in cheating one another. After being victimized, the master in this story commended the dishonest manager for his shrewd maneuvers, but the master's praise was not meant to be positive. Instead, it was given to communicate that people of faith should also use creativity, but it should be in ways that bring God glory. In our secular lives, we spend countless hours finding ways to advance our desires. If we expended just a small portion of this time to spiritual matters, we could align ourselves more with God's nature and will. Of course, this is not what we find in the world, even among Christians. Jesus, being well aware of the spiritual laziness within people, encourages us to prayerfully seek creative ways to move our lives to the next level. Our Christianity must not become static, but rather a journey that develops into Christ-likeness and service.

Jesus teaches how greed and secularism derail us from doing God's work. To emphasize this point, he said, "I tell you, use worldly wealth to gain friends for yourselves, that when it is gone, you will be welcomed into eternal dwellings (Luke 16:9). In other words, when we use our resources to help others, we not only make friends in this life, but this decreased focus on materialism will also enable us to attend to spiritual needs. The people we give to in this life may even welcome us in heaven, where money has no value. Those who give to the Lord's work, including a commitment to help the poor and needy, create bonds both on earth and in heaven. Only when our priority is God's kingdom and his righteousness, will we rid ourselves of the covetous and greed that imprisons our souls and brings God's wrath.

It is easy to get caught up in worldly things, thereby serving another master. Often subtle, this process takes us into a world, which excludes the Lord from our lives. If you were to develop a time-chart for every twenty-four-hour period, what would it reveal? How much time do you give to the Lord in devotion, study, prayer, worship, and service? When you think about it, we give most of our time to homes, other possessions, and entertainment—none of which have eternal value. In an effort to satisfy our emptiness, we continue seeking more things, and this involves covetousness and greed, the very sins that Jesus addresses in this parable.

While the neighborhood poor look to God for help, the Church is often guilty of material pursuits in their desire for elaborate buildings and artifacts. It is appalling how much wealth is held in church storehouses. How can any congregation or denomination preach the gospel, while at the same time continue to stockpile money and material assets beyond what is needed for emergency purposes? Equally disturbing, some clergy wear robes and related attire that cost thousands of dollars, while ignoring the needs of people in their community. Greed and deceit enters the holiest places with a shrewdness that blinds people to its reality. Churches involved in material abuse are not serving the Lord and his people, and their judgment is certain. Jesus alluded to this when he said, "If you have not been trustworthy in handling worldly wealth, who will trust you with true riches?"

Christ's teaching tells of a manager entrusted with the control of a rich man's affairs, but the rich man learned that the manager systematically robbed him. The story never reveals the manner in which the manager deceived his master, but it seems possible that the manager falsely reported transactions to his advantage. Without the record keeping that exists today, this deception could go undetected for a long time. But the rich man eventually discovered his manager's dishonest actions and terminated his services. Without a means for support, the manager devised another plan that continued his dishonest trend. Jesus tells us that the manager was not ready for physical labor, nor was he willing to beg for money. This led him to formulate a plan that made his master's debtors feel obligated to him. Having no employment, the manager hoped that the debtors would welcome him into their homes. The man who stole from his master would steal again, but now, others would participate in the scheme.

When Jesus taught this parable, the Jews could not charge interest from fellow Jews when they lent money, but like every rule in life, they found ways to get around it. They rationalized that these laws only addressed the poor because they should not be exploited, but if the transaction benefited both parties, the applied interest was acceptable. In the parable, the manager had the debtors rewrite their bonds to either eliminate the interest, or simply decrease the amount owed. This decrease benefited everyone but the rich man, who once again, found himself a victim.

As both a police officer and a prison chaplain, I have been amazed by the shrewdness of criminals and how they rationalize their acts. But prison inmates reflect society; therefore, they mirror the deception and greed found in our communities. Can you imagine the good that criminals could accomplish if they channeled their energy and creativity in positive ways? This is one of the missions of prison chaplaincy.

Concerned about his present and future security, the dishonest manager decided to walk in sin. In today's business world, corporate CEOs and others, through shrewd and deceptive practices, steal millions of dollars from the companies and employees they are paid to serve. One can find greed everywhere, and it is unlikely to disappear. From a spiritual perspective, those enslaved to wealth and power cannot serve God.

REFLECTION

• How much creative time do you give to God?

> We seldom think about creativity in the Christian context. Jesus told creative stories that employed nature and familiar things in life to manifest the truths of God, yet there seems to be little creativity in our churches. We should make every effort to bring creativity into the pulpits and educational programs of our ministries. It is creativity that brings the gospel message into a practical form.

• What does it mean to be God's steward? Has greed ever prevented you from serving the Lord?

> Christian stewardship means trusting in the Lord to meet all of our needs. In essence, it is allowing the Lord full control of the gifts that have been bestowed upon us. This includes tithing a portion of our income so that the church might continue to spread the gospel and engage in social ministries. When we find it difficult to tithe, we should examine the level of our faith in God's promises.

Twenty-Five

THE RICH MAN AND LAZARUS

Text: Luke 16:19–31 (NIV)

"There was a rich man who was dressed in purple and fine linen and lived in luxury every day. At his gate was laid a beggar named Lazarus, covered with sores and longing to eat what fell from the rich man's table. Even the dogs came and licked his sores. The time came when the beggar died and the angels carried him to Abraham's side. The rich man also died and was buried. In hell, where he was in torment, he looked up and saw Abraham far away, with Lazarus by his side. So he called to him, 'Father Abraham, have pity on me and send Lazarus to dip the tip of his finger in water and cool my tongue, because I am in agony in this fire.' But Abraham replied, 'Son, remember that in your lifetime you received your good things, while Lazarus received bad things, but now he is comforted here, and you are in agony. And besides all this, between us and you a great chasm has been fixed, so that those who want to go from here to you cannot, nor can anyone cross over from there to us.' He answered, 'Then I beg you, father, send Lazarus to my father's house, for I have five brothers. Let him warn them, so that they will not also come to this place of torment.' Abraham replied, 'They have Moses and the Prophets; let them listen to them.' 'No, father Abraham,' he said, 'but if someone from the dead goes to them, they will repent.' He said to him, 'If they do not listen to Moses and the Prophets, they will not be convinced even if someone rises from the dead.'"

One might wonder whether this parable is a true story. Unlike other lessons Jesus taught, this is the only instance where a proper name is used. He may have done this to personalize his teaching to give it more impact. But apart from this question, the lesson reveals graphic and penetrating insights into death and the afterlife.

The story has three characters who interact with each other. First, there is Lazarus the beggar, whose name in Hebrew, *Eleazer*, means *God has helped*. This name may bear some significance because the rich man refused to help this unfortunate person. Next, Jesus introduces the rich man who disregards Lazarus' desperate needs. In some translations, the rich man is called *Dives*, the Latin translation of *rich man*.[1] Both name translations cause some scholars to believe that this parable is an allegory. Considered the father of faith in the three monotheistic religions because of his absolute trust in God, Abraham is the third person found in the story. His faithfulness to God and his place in the heavenly realm is undisputed. Therefore, to be in Abraham's bosom or at his side is to be in God's presence.

In the previous parable, Jesus taught about the danger of loving money, emphasizing how greed and wealth often result in deceitful living and insensitivity toward others. Jesus, in this parable, focuses upon our responsibility and accountability before God as it relates to helping other people. Rather than a story pitting rich against the poor, this lesson is about stewardship and God's call to be compassionate toward those less fortunate. Regardless where we are in life, whether wealthy or with little means, we have the responsibility to respond to people who experience difficult times. However, this is only possible when we have a servant's heart filled with Christ's love.

This parable is a picture of how one's life on earth is directly connected to their death and eternal state. As such, we must understand how the early Jews thought about death and life beyond the grave. Death and resurrection are not clearly explained in one particular place in the Hebrew Bible, but we do find an unfolding revelation on this subject that culminates with the teachings of Jesus and his apostles. The apostle Paul provides us with most of what we consider today as orthodox theology on death and resurrection.

In early Jewish theology, *sheol* was the place where departed spirits went. Believed to be underground and known as the place of *shadows*, writers portray *sheol* as a miserable state, conveying some sense of punishment. Later, Jews thought *sheol* had two dimensions: one known as *hades*, or *hell*, where the wicked went and the other dimension called *paradise*, a tranquil place where one experienced God's peace and love.[2] The Jewish Talmud refers to the latter place as the state of bliss enjoyed by the faithful after their death. Implying intimacy, the Jews also called this place *Abraham's bosom*, coming from the ancient Jewish practice of reclining at meals, sometimes with one person's head resting on the bosom of another.

During the New Testament period, there was a general belief in an intermediate state of the departed, where both the righteous and the unrighteous awaited the Second Advent of Jesus Christ. The resurrection of the dead, the rapture of the living saints, God's final judgment and the ushering in of God's eternal kingdom are said to mark Christ's return. As seen in the parable, at the time of death, our spirit is either brought into God's realm to await a resurrected body, or it begins its eternal separation from God. In other words, at the time of death, one's eternal destiny is sealed.

Jesus' teachings make it clear that death removes any opportunity to change our minds and hearts about a relationship with God. The judgment will be a time when everyone reaps what they sowed in life, a point graphically illustrated in the afterlives of the rich man and Lazarus. When it comes to faithfully serving the Lord, there is no middle road. We either live in faith and walk in Christ's love or follow the path of self-will and unrighteousness. The Lord gives us every opportunity in this life to know him and be a servant in his kingdom. Therefore, on the day of judgment, we are without excuse.

As we examine the characters in this teaching, we learn that the rich man lived in splendor. His garments were purple, a color reflecting the upper class and royalty. In those days, linen came from flax found along the Nile River, which with the dyes used for clothing, were very expensive. This was particularly true of the purple dyes. In addition to the man's expensive clothing, he lived in a palace-sized home protected by a security gate. He owned the best of everything, and this granted him the privileges that typically accompany wealth. Seeing that his garbage was a feast for the poor, unnamed individuals took Lazarus to the rich man's front door. Unlike today, there were no agencies that assist the poor and needy. When no family members could provide help, the destitute often flocked to where the wealthy lived or gathered, hoping for sympathy.

Not only poor, Lazarus had a physical handicap, and sores covered his body. This was a common plight among the needy, because they lived in unclean conditions and could not acquire even basic health care. Jesus tells us that dogs licked Lazarus' sores as he lay at the rich man's gate. This sets the scene as the rich man passed by Lazarus to enter his huge estate. If Lazarus' presence upset the rich man, his displeasure existed because Lazarus intruded upon his privacy and sense of the good life, not because he felt compassion for the stricken man. When the needs of other people intrude upon our peaceful world, how do we react? Is it with sensitivity and compassion or out of some manner of obligation? Like the rich man in this story, there are times when the Church turns its back upon suffering that is found at its doorstep.

The death of both men is central to this lesson. First Lazarus died, and the rich man followed. The text mentions nothing about Lazarus being buried, for like most of the poor, he was probably carried to the city dump and burned with the trash. Even if Lazarus had friends, they had no money for a funeral. The rich man, however, was buried, and his funeral reflected his lifestyle, having all the rituals and praises of others. But as the parable vividly reveals, material wealth and accolades will not bring someone into God's realm. Over the years I have officiated at many funerals, participating in the rituals of the Church. I have also read obituaries which outline the lives and many accomplishments of the deceased. While these things are important and help family members get though a difficult loss, they will not change a person's destiny. What matters to God is the heart of the person and the life that they lived.

We learn that the angels carried Lazarus to Abraham's side, where he found comfort and renewal. What he lacked in his previous life was forever changed in the glory of God's presence. In contrast, the rich man found himself separated from God and in a place of torment. His mansion was left for others' enjoyment, and his purple robes were given to the moths. In his torment, he cried out for mercy. As Lazarus once begged for mercy, the rich man cried out to anyone who would listen, including Lazarus. He wanted Lazarus to place cool water on his tongue to help relieve his unquenchable thirst. Asking for Lazarus' help exhibits the rich man's desperation and state of hopelessness, but even if Lazarus wanted to help the man, the destiny of both men was already set. Abraham made it clear that neither man could cross over to where the other was.

When he realized that help was not forthcoming, the rich man focused on his brothers who still lived. If only someone would tell them about this horrible place, so that they might escape the same fate! This concern might make us believe that the rich man had a change of heart. Was this really the case, or was he trying to vindicate himself by claiming ignorance to God's teachings and his own conscience? Abraham responded quickly and told him that his brothers had the teachings of Moses and the Prophets, a benefit also given to the rich man during his life on earth. Perhaps, Abraham used this retort to expose the rich man's lame excuses. Taking his plea to another level, the rich man said that his brothers would certainly believe someone who was resurrected from the dead. Abraham answered that if his brothers refused to listen to Moses and the Prophets, they would not respond even if someone did return from the dead. These words speak of Jesus' resurrection, which was not believed by many people.

By society's standards, the rich man was a good person, respected by others as a leader in his community. In other words, no court of law would have convicted him of a crime, but God's court did convict him for his self-centered life and insensitivity toward those in need. He failed to see that God gave him his wealth for a purpose. A universal belief exists that what we possess is the result of our hard labor, thereby, we are the sole owners. People seldom think that God provides the opportunities that make our blessings possible, placing us in a position of responsibility and accountability. As Christians, God calls us to respond to those less fortunate, even when it requires sacrificial giving. This, however, is an unpopular lesson even among Christians. I have seldom heard church leaders voice concerns about needs within their communities. Normally, these topics are only discussed at certain times of the year, such as holidays. It usually falls upon pastors to keep these ministries alive.

Unconcerned about Lazarus' destitute state, the rich man saw him as an annoyance instead of being sensitive and empathetic toward his needs. If this were not the case, the rich man would have made some effort to help him. The text makes no mention that the rich man ever spoke to Lazarus, indicating that he ignored his presence, being all too familiar with the sight. How often do people, who profess the heart of Christ, turn away from the cries of those considered to be outcasts? Do we even pray for the sensitivity and compassion of Jesus Christ? Are the poor and sick welcomed into our lives and fellowships, or are they an annoyance and an embarrassment? I wonder how many churches have an active outreach to the less fortunate in their communities. Few church leaders even see our prisons as a mission field where God's grace is desperately needed. God calls us to the darkest places in life, but we tend to seek the most comfortable.

Like many people today, the rich man was full of excuses. If only this . . . if only that . . . If only someone warned him about the afterlife. This reaction is troubling because we should not respond out of fear, but rather a changed heart. If only someone explained God's teachings and how they relate to the poor and the sick. Even if the rich man was unfamiliar with God's teachings, what about his conscience? Although pride and self-will harden our hearts, we are aware of human suffering and know that we should somehow respond. Jesus teaches us that the more we have, the more that God requires of us (Luke 12:48). Although there are always exceptions, the wealthy normally have little to do with the lower class. Poverty is frequently viewed as a disease or plague that should be avoided.

REFLECTION

• How do you understand your responsibility to other people? Does your sensitivity to the needs of others result in concrete responses? Do you ever make excuses about helping people? How can you become a more caring person?

> We all belong to the human family, a truth which should move us to care for one another. It is not enough to talk about love and not put our words into action. Even sensitivity toward others means little without the concrete forms of ministry that improve life. We only become caring individuals when we get involved, going to those places of suffering and making a home there.

Twenty-Six

THE UNPROFITABLE SERVANTS

Text: Luke 17:7–10 (NIV)

> "Suppose one of you had a servant plowing or looking after the sheep. Would
> he say to the servant when he comes in from the field, 'Come along now and sit
> down to eat'? Would he not rather say, 'Prepare my supper, get yourself ready
> and wait on me while I eat and drink; after that you may eat and drink'? Would
> he thank the servant because he did what he was told to do? So you also, when
> you have done everything you were told to do, should say, 'We are unworthy
> servants; we have only done our duty.'"

This lesson provides insight into what it means to be a servant of the Lord.
The word *servant* is repeatedly found in the Hebrew Bible, relating to someone
who voluntarily serves another. The Scriptures also use the word to explain our
relationship with the Lord. The apostles claimed to be servants of God, as did
other followers of Christ. Jesus came to us as a humble servant, and he teaches
us that there is no higher calling than our service to God and humanity. Of
course, this concept is the antithesis of the world's definition of the word
servant. Rather than being a spiritual calling to serve God and walk in the
teachings of Christ, society perceives servants as inferior individuals of low
societal standing.

Jesus taught this parable to provide perspective and to solicit self-
examination. Being a servant of the Lord addresses how we understand ourselves and our purpose in life. It also speaks to the spirit and manner in which
we should serve. A humble life, void of pride and self-will, is absolute if we are
to share in our Savior's nature and his mission to humanity. True servants of

the Lord place others above themselves and never seek praise for their works. Their service to God and others is a natural response to their lives in Jesus Christ. Jesus came to us in human flesh, a servant to all people, sharing in our joys and sorrows and offering up his life for our sins. If Jesus sacrificed everything for us, how can we do less? If we claim to be followers of Jesus, we are followers of his teachings and example.

I have met many wonderful servants of God, individuals from different backgrounds and ages, who have been living examples for me. They were people of quiet faith with pure hearts, who sought no attention or recognition for their faithful and compassionate service. On the other hand, I also encountered those who constantly needed praise for what they accomplished. If these folks only knew the poor example they set and how their attitudes harm the Church's work!

If we give our lives to the Lord, we acknowledge his ownership and providence. As the apostle Paul tells us, this means offering ourselves up our total lives to the Lord (Romans 12:1, 2). As we surrender ourselves to God, we take on his divine qualities, which results in an obedience emanating out of love. Our service is not manufactured, nor do we serve out of a sense of obligation. Instead, our service is the result of God's grace in us.

I always encouraged my parishioners to take up the Cross of Jesus Christ. Some insights I provided are found in *The Beauty of Caring* by Lloyd Ogilvie. In his book, Ogilvie shares thoughts on what it means to be God's servant. He lists five important elements:

We are Impelled.
We are impelled because Christ meets our own needs, and this moves us to touch the lives of others.

We Identify
Servants do not serve at a safe distance. They feel another's pain and suffering as if it were their own. When God came to us through Christ, he did not give lofty advice. He became one of us.

We Intercede
Prayers of intervention not only unleash the power of God in another person's life, but they also clarify what the Lord wants to say to that person. The intensity of our caring must be focused so that it meets the person's deepest need.

We are Involved
We must listen to others and dare to enter their situation. It is easy to tell others what to do but difficult to get into their skin and feel their anguish, fear, or frustration. People need to feel intense empathy.

We are Incisive in Introducing People to the Savior
Many people help others with physical or emotional suffering but leave them
    with an eternal problem. As servants, we must help others heal spiritually.[1]

The compassion of Jesus speaks to the whole person, a truth which is clearly demonstrated in his earthly ministry. The healing he performed, including those whom he raised from the dead, give us insight into his empathy and selfless nature. He reached out to every manner of sickness and disease, with an unconditional love that shocked some people. His cures on the Sabbath violated the law, often resulting in stern responses. Jesus' caring and miraculous power were well-known by the masses, to such an extent that people traveled long distances with the hope of being healed. The miracles, not only affirmed his divine anointing, but they also revealed a loving God to the people. Rather than a deity who simply wrote unrealistic laws that could not be obeyed, in Jesus they found love and encouragement. When Jesus told his listeners that he and the Father were one, hope became a reality in their lives.

Although our Savior's healing ministry resulted from his love, it served to bring God's kingdom to the people. This was the reason for the incarnation, his earthly mission and passion. While he could not pass by human suffering, his higher purpose was to offer the people forgiveness and eternal life. As the Lord's servants of mercy, we are also called to a suffering world, but we must never neglect bringing people to Jesus Christ, who heals the soul and gives eternal life. Like our Savior's ministry, our commission is the healing of both body and soul. To heal the body and disregard the soul is to leave a person in a state of darkness and without hope.

As the parable emphasizes, we should have the mind and the heart of a servant, which enables us to identify and bond with people. This is God's will as seen in the life of Jesus Christ. God calls the Church to be a priesthood, serving as intercessors for one another through prayer and an active ministry of presence. Being God's servant is not a part-time situation, nor does it simply involve isolated acts of kindness or a sense of duty. Instead, it is a life given to God and the humanity for whom Jesus gave his life.

The parable speaks about a servant who came in from a day's work in the field, but he did not stop working. Instead of the master of the house preparing the servant's supper, the servant continued his work for the master. His service did not end after a day in the field. What a lesson for us! As the Lord's servants, we never cease giving ourselves to God and one another. Serving God is not always a matter of observable works or deeds. It is a life transformed by love, and this speaks to the whole person and how we respond and interact to the world around us. In essence, it is directly related to who we are in Jesus Christ.

REFLECTION

- Does your life reflect the heart and mind of a servant? Explain the struggles you have in being a servant.

  Being a servant is a life that even mature Christians find difficult. Although we desire to serve God and one another, we find ourselves struggling to maintain a servant attitude and lifestyle. As previously stated, pride and self-centeredness must continuously be resisted if we are to serve the Lord in the spirit of love. Personal reflection at the end of each day will make us aware of our shortcomings, thereby revealing the areas that require prayer and spiritual discipline. Learning how to listen to God and each other is another avenue that creates the humility of a servant.

- Have you ever sought recognition for the things you have done?

  What person does not want to be recognized in one way or another? This is a natural characteristic and even important for one's emotional development. The concern comes when this need controls our personality and how we relate to others. It can also be detrimental to our spiritual life. Persistently asking God for humility and focusing upon the sacrificial life of Christ, the apostles and the saints of the Church, helps us maintain focus on the virtues of holiness.

- Do you ever serve God out of a sense of obligation or fear?

  To serve the Lord out of a sense of obligation is analogous to paying someone for their services. We serve God because his love has changed our lives, giving us a heart that is filled with gratitude and praise. Instead of living in fear and judgment, we revere the Shepherd of our life, desiring to share in his nature and will.

- Are there boundaries in your service to God and others?

  When we seek God and the leading of the Holy Spirit, boundaries do not exist, unless our serving becomes questionable, which may require more prayer and time for answers. Care should be taken that we not move ahead of the Lord. People often allow their own desires to replace God's will. When it comes to love, there are no boundaries, but caution is always necessary when helping people.

- Is your church emphasizing the importance of being a servant?

  The emphasis upon being a servant is a theme which is found throughout the Scriptures, and most churches do communicate this in their teachings. However, we should be challenged to put this teaching into practice. This can be accomplished through church and community involvement.

Twenty-Seven

THE PERSISTENT WIDOW

Text: Luke 18:1–8 (NIV)

> Then Jesus told his disciples a parable to show them that they should always pray and not give up. He said: "In a certain town there was a judge who neither feared God nor cared about men. And there was a widow in that town who kept coming to him with the plea, 'Grant me justice against my adversary.' For some time he refused. But finally he said to himself, 'Even though I don't fear God or care about men, yet because this widow keeps bothering me, I will see that she gets justice, so that she won't eventually wear me out with her coming!'" And the Lord said, "Listen to what the unjust judge says. And will not God bring about justice for his chosen ones, who cry out to him day and night? Will he keep putting them off? I tell you, he will see that they get justice, and quickly. However, when the Son of Man comes, will he find faith on the earth?"

This lesson was specifically given to Jesus' disciples. On the surface, the content and message appears to be similar to the parable of the *Friend at Midnight*, in which Jesus addresses the importance of being persistent in prayer. Persistence is also a theme in this teaching, but another emphasis is God's justice. While absolute justice is not a reality in this life, most people resolutely seek some manner of justice when they are treated unfairly.

Over the years, I wrote a few letters to companies in an attempt to correct personal injustices. The most recent was related to an airline ticket to Athens, Greece, which I had to cancel due to an impending surgery. I made numerous telephones calls, being transferred from one person and department to another without any success. You can imagine the nightmare! Success finally came when an airline supervisor checked her computer and noted how many calls I made without resolving the problem. She also knew that I documented the agents' names I conversed with, and she realized that my persistence would continue. Needless to say, it was not long before there was a mutual solution. I have learned that regardless of the injustice, it is persistence that solves problems. This, of course, is a process that can bring intense frustration, and possibly anger. Everywhere we look, we find some type of injustice, to such an extent that many people simply accept what comes their way. As society becomes more complex and impersonal, the problem increases.

Jesus knew that his disciples would suffer injustices as they began to spread the gospel. Because of their faith, they became victims of unyielding persecution. In fact, according to tradition, eleven of the twelve apostles were martyred for their faith and evangelism. Exiled to the island of Patmos, the apostle John was the only survivor. Knowing their futures, Jesus taught his followers the importance of being persistent in their prayer life. He told them to continuously pray for justice, both for themselves and for the Church. Jesus emphasized that spiritual weakness comes when one ceases to pray in the midst of trials.

Sometimes, our greatest struggles with prayer come when we need prayer the most. The emotional upset accompanying life's trials often results in a defeatist attitude. We must confront this attitude with God's Word and his promises found in scripture. In the wilderness, Jesus gained victory over Satan by standing upon the Word of God. It was his faith and communion with the Father that defeated evil. We often allow our emotions to take control of our lives, when what we need is the faith that keeps us persistently praying. There are times when negative emotions consume us, but we must not allow these emotions to keep us from communion with the Lord. This is particularly true when we are victims of injustice. Whatever the trial, God promises us his sustaining grace, keeping us strong until the time when we are set free from all injustice.

According to Mosaic Law, judges were to give special attention to widows, primarily because of their dependence upon men. When the husband died, widows were left at the mercy of relatives and the eldest son to provide for them. God claimed a special interest in widows, even referring to himself as their husband (Psalm 68:5; 146:9). The Lord condemned those who intentionally defrauded or oppressed widows (Psalm 94:6; Ezekiel 22:7; Malachi 3:5). In the apostolic church, widows received assistance from the people when their family members were not supportive (Acts 6:1; James 1:27). The apostle Paul encouraged families to live their faith by supporting widows who were related to them (I Timothy 5:3–16). Most widows were defenseless, poor, and targets of oppression and fraud. Apparently, this was the widow's situation in our lesson. She had no advocate to speak on her behalf, which left her in a hopeless state. But rather than giving up, she was relentless in her pursuit of justice. The unrighteous judge finally gave in to her plea because he knew that she would not stop coming to him until she received justice.

If an unrighteous judge eventually responds to someone's plea for justice, how much more will God respond to his children who continuously call upon him? This is the message that Jesus wanted to communicate to his disciples. He told them to have faith and be patient, knowing that God would provide the strength to overcome injustice. The apostle John told the Christians throughout Asia Minor that Christ's power in us is greater than the power of injustice (I John 4:4). God promises us that he will never leave or forsake us, and this promise is realized through faith and prayer.

In the parable's last verse, Jesus asked his disciples if there will be faith on earth when he returns. But since this was not a question that could be answered, it was an emphasis on the need for faith in the midst of trials and persecution. Even when life's circumstances became overwhelming, the disciples were to trust in God's wisdom and providence. This same message is also for us, especially during those times when our lives seem to be falling apart. Life's difficulties put our faith to the test, and prayer is crucial for victory. While praying for justice is a personal matter, it is also seeking the kingdom of God in the hearts of people. In the final analysis, the Lord is the judge of every person, and his justice will be eternally realized when Jesus returns.

REFLECTION

- How do you define justice as it relates to this parable? Why does Jesus tell us to persistently pray for justice?

  We normally think of injustice in terms of a particular act or life situation, but history reveals the many forms encountered by individuals and societies. The historical Church has certainly wielded its power in unjust ways, and in the world of politics injustice has many faces. Only when Jesus returns will true justice become a reality. In the meantime, God provides his people with the grace that brings them through life's trials. This is the justice that the nonbeliever does not experience.

- How do the trials of life affect your prayer life? Provide some examples in your response.

  Life's trials can either draw people closer to the Lord or cause them to lose faith. No one had more trials than the apostle Paul, who learned that God's power is manifested in the midst of our weaknesses and trials. In other words, when in faith, we completely open our lives to God, we receive the fullness of his grace. Although the Lord's grace is always with us, it is during those difficult times when we realize his power and grace more fully. We were never promised a trouble-free life, but we are promised God's transforming and sustaining grace. Our prayer life is incomplete if we do not seek the grace that sustains us.

Twenty-Eight

THE PHARISEE AND THE TAX COLLECTOR

Text: Luke 18:9–14 (NIV)

> To some who were confident of their own righteousness and looked down on everybody else, Jesus told this parable: "Two men went up to the temple to pray, one a Pharisee and the other a tax collector. The Pharisee stood up and prayed about himself: 'God, I thank you that I am not like other men—robbers, evil doers, adulterers—or even like this tax collector. I fast twice a week and give a tenth of all I get.' But the tax collector stood at a distance. He would not even look up to heaven, but beat his breast and said, 'God, have mercy on me, a sinner.' I tell you that this man, rather than the other, went home justified before God. For everyone who exalts himself will be humbled, and he who humbles himself will be exalted."

Jesus told this parable for the benefit of those who were confident of their righteousness and saw others as inferior to them. Although he obviously directed this lesson at the religious leaders, its message was not limited to only them. In this contrast between the prayers of the Pharisee and the tax collector, Jesus addresses his repeated message of denouncing self-righteousness and pride. While this illustration provides insights into prayer and how we should approach God, the primary teaching relates to one's character and how arrogance prevents us from having a pure-hearted relationship with God and one another. In this succinct lesson, Jesus shows us the lives of two individuals, how they view themselves, and the way this impacts their spirituality.

Jesus wanted his listeners to know that we are all sinners in need of God's continuing forgiveness.

The Pharisee stood before God and gave thanks for the gifts that made him superior to others, which included the tax collector praying nearby. Believing to be free of sin, he spoke to God with an arrogant pride. Instead of seeking the Lord's mercy for his sins, he tried to impress God with his high position and good works. He told God that he fasted twice a week and tithed a tenth of what he earned. Since the Law only required one fast on the yearly Day of Atonement, the Pharisee wanted God to know the extent of his spiritual sacrifices.

In contrast, the tax collector came before God with a humble and penitent heart, acknowledging that he was a sinner in need of mercy. He beat his chest in emotional anguish, and his sorrow and guilt made him unable to lift his head. His prayer revealed an honest self-examination and the lifting up of his soul. Rather than spouting religious rhetoric, his communion with God was an invitation for divine cleansing and spiritual renewal. As Jesus noted, God forgave the tax collector, not the Pharisee.

King David wrote one of the most profound prayers in scripture. In Psalm 25, he prayed: "To you, O Lord, I lift up my soul; in you I trust, O my God. Remember, O Lord, your great mercy and love, for they are from of old. For the sake of your name, O Lord, forgive my iniquity, though it is great The Lord confides in those who fear him; he makes his covenant known to them" (1, 6, 11, 14).

David's prayer reveals his intense guilt and his desire for the cleansing that comes through repentance. His words, which reflect his soul searching, prove to be a stumbling block for many people Yet, God already knows our needs before we pray, and to be less than honest is deception (I Chronicles 28:9; Jeremiah 17:10). We grow up in a world of half-truths, denial and deception, and these sins become infused in our nature. We must confront these areas if we want to grow in Jesus Christ. David asked God to search out his heart and try his thoughts for wickedness within. By doing this, he solicited a divine probe of his inner life, including those dark and unconscious areas (Psalm 139:23, 24).

Regardless how far we have traveled in our spiritual walk, our righteousness comes through the redemptive work of Jesus Christ. The prophet Isaiah wrote, "All of us have become like one who is unclean, and all our righteous acts are like filthy rags; we all shrivel up like a leaf, and like the wind our sins sweep us away" (Isaiah 64:6). The apostle Paul told the Galatians that if righteousness is gained by the law, then Christ died for nothing. Paul also said that it was no longer he who lived but rather, Christ living in him (Galatians 2:20, 21). Although we continue to strive for holiness, we realize that only God's grace can save us. In the midst of our weaknesses is a merciful Savior who is our intercessor before the Father.

The Lord only accepts a humble and contrite heart, and apart from his forgiveness there is no salvation. I met people who believe that they are without sin, concluding that their good works are sufficient to bring them into God's kingdom. They fail to understand the many facets of sin within the context of thoughts, words, and deeds. These same people fail to comprehend that the good in them comes from God. Unfortunately, there are religious communities that manifest this same attitude, believing that God's truth belongs only to them. This divisiveness often prevents Christians from different backgrounds and cultures from coming together for mutual encouragement, support, and service. These groups also diminish the witness and power of the universal Church, which creates obstacles to the gospel message of love, forgiveness, and equality in Jesus Christ. Without a servant's heart that promotes peace and unity, we become our own worst enemies.

Communion with God and one another requires the humility and honesty exemplified in the tax collector. Although this may be initially painful, the Lord can only help us when we rid ourselves of pride. We find the ultimate example of humility in our Savior, who left his heavenly glory to become one of us. Concerning Jesus, we should engrave Paul's words to the Philippians into our hearts. He wrote: "Your attitude should be the same as that of Christ Jesus: Who, being in very nature God, did not consider equality with God something to be grasped, but made himself nothing, taking the very nature of a servant, being made in human likeness. And being found in appearance as a man, he humbled himself and became obedient to death—even death on a cross!" (Philippians 2:5–8).

Knowing that it was soon time to leave this world, Jesus spent time with his disciples, giving them words of encouragement. On one occasion, he wrapped a towel around his waist, poured water in a basin, and began washing his disciples' feet. While illustrating the cleansing power of his imminent death, this act also served as an example of the humility by which the disciples should serve. After the foot washing, Jesus said, "I have set an example, that you should do as I have done" (John 13:1–17). As a reflection of society, the Church experiences the tensions between worldly and spiritual influences. We teach about the humility of Christ and the example this provides, but living the life is quite different. It requires that inner cleansing that the apostle Paul refers to as the circumcision of the heart.

REFLECTION

- How do you understand your life in Jesus Christ? Have you ever considered yourself superior to other people? If so, explain the circumstances.

  An honest person will admit to occasional feelings of superiority. Regardless of where we are in life, we sometimes make comparisons and judgments that produce these feelings and attitudes. We find this in many forms, including race, religion, and cultural backgrounds. Superior attitudes are also seen in our treatment of the elderly, the disabled and those living at the lower end of the socioeconomic ladder.

- Do you pray for humility and a pure heart? Are your prayers an honest reflection of your inner life?

  There is no benefit to prayer unless we approach the Lord with a pure and contrite heart. Without humility and honesty before God, we compound our sins by communicating arrogance and dishonesty before the throne of grace. When we fail to acknowledge and confess our sins, we close the door to reconciliation.

Twenty-Nine

THE TEN MINAS

Text: Luke 19:11–27 (NIV)

While they were listening to this, he went on to tell them a parable, because he was near Jerusalem and the people thought that the kingdom of God was going to appear at once. He said: "A man of noble birth went to a distant country to have himself appointed king and then to return. So he called ten of his servants and gave them ten minas. 'Put this money to work,' he said, 'until I come back.' But his subjects hated him and sent a delegation after him to say, 'We don't want this man to be our king.' He was made king, however, and returned home. Then he sent for the servants to whom he had given the money, in order to find out what they had gained with it. The first one came and said, 'Sir, your mina has earned ten more.' 'Well done, my good servant!' his master replied. 'Because you have been trustworthy in a very small matter, take charge of ten cities.' The second came and said, 'Sir, your mina has earned five more.' His master answered, 'You take charge of five cities.' Then another servant came and said, 'Sir, here is your mina; I have kept it laid away in a piece of cloth. I was afraid of you, because you are a hard man. You take out what you did not put in and reap what you did not sow.' His master replied, 'I will judge you by your own words, you wicked servant! You knew, did you, that I am a hard man, taking out what I did not put in, and reaping what I did not sow? Why then didn't you put my money on deposit, so that when I came back, I could have collected it with interest?' Then he said to those standing by, 'Take his mina away from him and give it to the one who has ten minas.' 'Sir,' they said, 'he already has ten!' He replied, 'I tell you that to everyone who has, more will be given, but as for the one who has nothing, even what he has will be taken away.

> But those enemies of mine who did not want me to be king over them—bring them here and kill them in front of me.'"

Except for a few differences, this parable's content is similar to the one given in Matthew 25:14–30. According to Luke, Jesus shared this teaching while at the house of Zacchaeus, a chief tax collector and wealthy man. The setting is Jericho, about seventeen miles from Jerusalem, and he taught this parable during the Passover. Jesus was on his way to the temple in Jerusalem, with his ministry on earth close to an end. Every Passover was met with the spirit of Messianic expectation, primarily because many people believed that during this holiday God would send the Messiah to deliver them from the Romans. This concept derived from the nature of the holiday, which celebrated Israel's deliverance from Egypt. The Passover was always a time of excitement, when the Jews looked to God's promise for an anointed deliverer. In fact, the excitement became so intense that additional Roman soldiers were brought into Jerusalem to quell and help subdue the frenzy. I have been in Jerusalem during the Passover and witnessed the excitement on the streets.

Knowing the people's expectation and their false understanding of God's kingdom, Jesus told this parable to correct their thinking. Although the Jews had different ideas about the Messiah, most believed that his appearance would result in a worldly kingdom that would restore Israel's freedom and glory. Zacchaeus, who climbed a tree to see Jesus among the large crowd gathered around him, probably believed this as well. Little did Zacchaeus know that the Son of God would soon be his house guest.

Although Matthew's account of this parable varies somewhat from Luke's version, both have parallel truths relating to investing our lives and using our gifts for the Lord. Luke, however, describes a nobleman receiving a kingdom and how his subjects respond to his royal appointment. This nobleman is Jesus, who, after his ministry on earth, returned to heaven to receive his kingdom. The reference to a *distant country* relates to his ascension and return to the Father. During his absence, we should invest our talents for the work of the kingdom. The different amounts given by the nobleman reflect the various gifts that God gives us to invest for him. When the nobleman returned, he called his servants together to give an account. This analogy represents the certainty of Jesus' return when everyone will give an account of their lives.

In the story, two of the three men made sound investments for the nobleman. They modestly reported the increase, and the nobleman commended them for what they had done. Boasting about the increase would have been inappropriate because the investments were made with the nobleman's money, and they did only what their master expected of them. The third man did not acquire any interest. Instead, like many people today, he hid what was supposed to be invested. As a result, the nobleman gave the third man's mina to the one who proved himself worthy by having the best return amount. This tells us that those who do not invest their gifts will lose what God gave them. When we refuse to invest our lives for God, he will find others who are willing. This is evident both in our daily lives and in church ministry. The individuals who refuse God's plan for their lives ultimately lose the opportunities that bring fulfillment and purpose.

The disobedient servant excused himself, referring to his master as a severe and demanding person, but the nobleman refused to accept his excuse and used the servant's own words to condemn him. The servant's response obviously disclosed resentment toward his master. Why should he be required to make an investment for someone who reaps benefits without doing the work? People today often have a similar attitude, believing that their efforts lack satisfaction and rewards. Why work for the Lord? What is in it for me? The resentment toward God and his expectations of us are certainly found in the Church, where self-centeredness still exists. Many people, who consider themselves spiritual, refuse to serve God unless they reap some personal benefit. This includes individuals who have been affiliated with the Church all of their lives. Somehow, they rewrite the gospel message to suit their own purposes.

The parable has a stark and frightening conclusion. The nobleman ordered that the men considered his enemies, who rejected his royal appointment, be put to death. A distinction is made between the servant who failed to make an investment and those who did not want the nobleman as their king. Although God will confront the sins of his servants, Christ's real enemies are the people who refuse his Lordship over their lives and openly speak out against him. These individuals will experience the second death mentioned in the Scriptures, the eternal separation from God's love.

REFLECTION

- Have you completely accepted the Lordship of Jesus Christ? Are there any areas in your life that have not been turned over to God?

  When we receive Jesus Christ into our lives, there is a spiritual birth that takes place. However, like an infant born into the world, our growth process has just begun. This reality must always be considered when personal discouragement surfaces, and also when looking at the lives of other Christians. But like a young child who struggles for maturity, our goal is continuous growth in the Lord. It is through the sanctifying process that we progressively give more of ourselves to God.

- In what ways have you made investments for the Lord? If Jesus were to return today, what would he say to you?

  If the desire of our heart is pure, and we have made every effort to serve God and walk in faith, then our Creator will assuredly give us his eternal blessings.

Thirty

CONCLUSION

You just completed a brief spiritual journey, which hopefully deepened your understanding of our Savior's teachings and how they speak to your life. When we internalize the words of Jesus, we begin to take on his nature and share in his love and mission for all people. This was my purpose for writing on the parables.

As you have noticed, the topics in our Lord's teachings have both connecting and similar themes. In reading the Scriptures, we find that Jesus emphasized and repeated the truths that are crucial to our discipleship. With different stories, his objective was to imprint essential truths upon our hearts and minds, challenging us to a life that is filled with joy, purpose and hope.

Authors do not write devotional books simply to be read once and then placed on a shelf. The words of Christ should serve as a continuing source of spiritual food and reflection that enables us to draw close to our Savior. Growing in Jesus Christ requires a spiritual diet, and there is no better food than the parables he told. The continued study of our Lord's teachings will reveal the deep and wonderful truths that will stir your heart and bring you into his love.

APPENDIX:
PARABLE STUDY SHEET

Title:

Text:

The Setting and Circumstances for the Teaching:

The Primary Theme and Message:

Key Words and Passages:

Characters in the Lesson:

Symbolism Used:

Personal Application and Message for the Church:

NOTES

INTRODUCTION

1. *New International Version of the Bible* (Grand Rapids, MI: Zondervan Corporation, 1979), Preface, p. vii.

CHAPTER NINE

1. David A. Redding, *The Parables He Told* (New York: Harper & Row Publishers, 1976), p. 135.

CHAPTER TWELVE

1. Merrill F. Unger, *Unger's Bible Dictionary* (Chicago, IL: Moody Press, 1966), pp. 698–699.

CHAPTER THIRTEEN

1. Merrill F. Unger, *Unger's Bible Dictionary* (Chicago, IL: Moody Press, 1966), p. 725.

CHAPTER TWENTY-FIVE

1. William Smith, *Smith's Bible Dictionary* (Philadelphia, PA: A. J. Holman & Co., 1896), pp. 77, 178.
2. Ibid., pp. 119–120.

CHAPTER TWENTY-SIX

1. Lloyd Ogilvie, *The Beauty of Caring* (Eugene, OR: Harvest House Publishers, 1981), pp. 32–33. Taken from *The Beauty of Caring* by Lloyd John Ogilvie. Copyright © 1981 by Harvest House Publishers, Eugene, OR. Used by Permission, www.harvesthousepublishers.com

RESOURCES

Alexander, David, and Pat, eds. *Eerdman's Handbook to the Bible*. Grand Rapids, MI: William B. Eerdmans Publishing Company, 1978.

Bonhoeffer, Dietrich. *Christ the Center*. San Francisco, CA: Harper Collins Publishers, 1978.

Goguel, Maurice. *Jesus and the Origins of Christianity*, Vol. II. New York: Harper Torchbooks, 1960.

Harrison, Everett F. *Baker's Dictionary of Theology*. Grand Rapids, MI: Baker Book House, 1960.

Heick, O. W. *History of Protestant Theology*. Philadelphia, PA: The Muhlenberg Press, 1946.

Küng, Hans. *The Church*. Garden City, NY: Image Books, 1976.

Morgan, G. Campbell. *The Parables and Metaphors of Our Lord*. Old Tapan, NJ: Fleming H. Revell Company, 1943.

Nave, Orville J., ed. *Nave's Topical Bible*. Milford, NJ: Mott Media, Inc., 1984.

Ogilvie, Lloyd John. *The Beauty of Caring*. Eugene, OR: Harvest House Publishers, 1981.

Paul, Leslie. *Son of Man*. New York: E. P. Dutton & Co., Inc, 1961.

Peterson, Eugene H. *Stories of Jesus*. Colorado Springs, CO: Navpress, 1999.

Redding, David A. *The Parables He Told*. New York: Harper and Row Publishers, 1976.

Ridderbos, Herman. *Paul, An Outline of His Theology*. Grand Rapids, MI: William B. Eerdmans Publishing Company, 1979.

Rushdoony, Rousas. *The Institutes of Biblical Laws*. Dallas, TX: The Craig Press, 1973.

Smith, William. *Smith's Bible Dictionary*. Philadelphia, PA: A. J. Holman and Company, 1980.

144   *Resources*

Sowney, David G., ed. *The Abingdon Bible Commentary*. New York: Abingdon Press, 1929.

Strauss, Lehman. *The Book of Revelation*. Neptune, NJ: Loizeaux Brothers, 1964.

Taylor, William M. *The Parables of Our Savior*. Grand Rapids, MI: Kregel Publications, 1975.

Turner, H. E. W. *Jesus, Master and Lord*. New York: A. R. Mowbray & Company, Limited, 1954.

Unger, Merrill F. *Unger's Bible Dictionary*. Chicago, IL: Moody Press, 1987.

Young, Robert. *Young's Analytical Concordance to the Bible*. Grand Rapids, MI: William B. Eerdmans Publishing Company, 1964.

About the Author

HENRY G. COVERT is an ordained minister with the United Church of Christ. He is the author of *Ministry to the Incarcerated* and has served as Adjunct Professor at Pennsylvania State University.